Ñ

THE SHAPING FORCES IN MUSIC

An Inquiry Into the Nature of

Harmony · Melody · Counterpoint · Form

By

ERNST TOCH

CRITERION MUSIC CORP.

R.K.O. Building, New York

To the country which gave me shelter when shelter was taken from me I dedicate this book in everlasting gratitude.

I do not know—no composer does—by whom my music is going to be liked, by whom disliked, by whom met with indifference. But having lived here long enough to know my fellow citizens' hunger both for music and education I may perhaps hope that this book will reach and help also some of those whom my music will not reach or affect.

I wish I could convey that this dedication is not a mere gesture. Life and work were put back into my hands when they were doomed for me to cease. With this awareness, and with the awareness also that whatever I have created since then and may still create is rightfully this country's, I presume to offer this dedication. May the book return in humble service and usefulness a fraction of what I have received.

E. T.

PREFACE

This book contains a compilation of observations and ideas which have accumulated through years of experience as a composer and teacher.

It attempts to bring out and emphasize the timeless and permanent features of music as against the time-bound and transient ones. In doing so it attempts to reconcile the at-times-"classical" with the at-times-"modern."

It is intended for those who may have gone through a certain amount of elementary music theory, say the fundamentals of traditional harmony as they are commonly taught, and may find themselves at odds with prevailing traits of that music which does not correspond to this knowledge. Presupposing such knowledge of the elements, the book does not stop to explain them, or to explain the terms which, if necessary, can be easily found in any music dictionary. It rather concentrates on material not incorporated in the current textbooks.

It is also intended for music lovers who desire to attain a better understanding—"appreciation"—of music at large; for practical musicians and amateurs who are aware of the incompleteness of their musical upbringing when confronted with a more progressive type of music; and finally for all those interested in trying their hand at musical composition. Thus it may well serve as a vade mecum for instruction or for self-instruction.

In the course of time, musical theory has developed certain divisions of detached analysis and study, such as harmony, counterpoint and so on, and has treated them individually. The division of theory into these branches is admissible only if we never, from beginning to end, lose sight of the close inter-relationship of the disciplines and their constant reciprocal influence and inter-dependence.

There is another item, fundamental enough to be put down at the outset and to be always kept in mind:

Beware of pedantry! Art resists any pedantic approach just as nature does. Neither art nor nature knows an unqualified "It must" or "It must not".

In art, as in nature, forces are at work which hardly ever —probably never—manifest themselves in pure, unbroken appearance; although the knowledge of their pure, unbroken appearance is necessary to understand the better their concourse and conflict. And even if we think we have caught everything we are at any time apt to encounter a freak which catches us by baffling and perhaps refreshing surprise.

In art and nature alike our knowledge is based primarily on observation of existing phenomena. In art and nature alike first comes creation; then, second in sequence, comes theory trying to describe and to explain. However, this sequence does not preclude that theory, in putting together its observations and drawing conclusions, may also by way of speculation and development pave the way for new discoveries or anticipate future events.

In pursuit of the principle that theoretical knowledge rests on observation of the existing, the ideas laid down in this book are exemplified almost exclusively by quotations from the living music literature of the past and the present. They are not intended to invite the student to copy and imitate. They are intended to stimulate his imagination and to inspire his own searching, discerning and, eventually, creative faculties.

In presenting this book to the music student at large, I wish to acknowledge that its formation owes much to the keen interest and the searching inquiries of my students over the years. The ultimate impulse to put my ideas down in the present form came from the response I received to a lecture series "The Shaping Forces in Music", delivered at Harvard University in fall 1944.

In the actual preparation of the book for publication, I am indebted to Dr. Max Krone and Robert Trotter for their valuable suggestions, and most of all to Dr. Gerald Strang for his able assistance in the final revision of the manuscript.

CONTENTS

HARMONY

MELODY

COUNTERPOINT

FORM

HARMONY

«Πάντα ῥεῖ»
(*Everything is in flux*)

Heraclitus

CHAPTER I

HARMONY AND CHORD

"Harmony" is the technical term for the coincidence of three or more different pitches.

So is "Chord".

This seems to imply that the two terms are identical.

Yet they are not; though in certain instances they may well be used for each other.

The symbols of Ex. 1, for example,

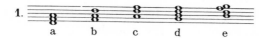

stand unequivocally for certain chords: *a* for triad, *b* and *c* for its two inversions (6-chord and $^6_4$-chord respectively), *d* for 7-chord, *e* for its first inversion ($^6_5$-chord). Yet they do not convey anything in the matter of *sound*, meaning *harmony*. They are like empty honeycombs, waiting to be filled with substance; dead skeletons in need of being awakened to life.

Any of the symbols of Ex. 2, put before them, will perform this transmutation.

1

Only now the symbols of Ex. 1 become unequivocally indicative of their sounds; only now the chords become *harmonies*. And though remaining the same chords — triad, 6-chord, 7-chord, etc. — they become different harmonies according to the application of the several clues of Ex. 2, **a-d**.

Bars 1 and 2 of Ex. 3 show a series of equal chords (6-chords) with constantly changing harmonies:

whereas Ex. 3a shows, with a single exception marked +, one unchanged harmony (the harmony of the *c* major tonic triad) in a series of changing chords:

We begin to sense that harmony is the far superior, far more relevant notion. It certainly is easier for the ear to distinguish two different harmonies than two different chord structures. It becomes evident that harmony has a greater bearing upon composition at large than chord; that harmony—not chord—may constitute part of the personal characteristics of different composers (Wagner, Debussy) ; that harmony, even within the same composition, has greater functional significance than chord. And it is finally safe to say that the functional significance of the chord recedes in the same measure as composition withdraws from the keybound, tone-center-bound, degree-bound idiom of classical music, until, in completely a-tonal music, the chord-function practically vanishes to zero as compared with the harmony-function.

Still, while the functional value of the chord, even in classical music, is so much inferior to that of the harmony, it is present all the same.

To give a simple example: In the following cadential clause (Ex. 4a):

so familiar to us from countless occurrences that it hardly pays to select a special quotation, the two figured chords obviously reveal their harmonic identity. Yet they could not exchange their places (as shown in Ex. 4b) because of the definite *functional* (in this case cadential) mission of either chord.

Suppose we were to harmonize a simple phrase like the one of Ex. 5 in a simple way.

The folk tune offers, as most folk tunes do, for its most natural harmonization the use of the three basic harmonies I (tonic), V (dominant) and IV (sub-dominant):

Yet, planted there bluntly in their root positions (Ex. 6), the effect of these harmonies, correct as they are in themselves, would be rude as compared with Ex. 7.

Here the harmonies are the same, yet they partly exhibit an inverted chordal structure (6-chords in bars 2 and 3). In Ex. 6 the harmonies answer solely the several subsections opposite which they appear and to which they give the inherent harmonic support; yet they are wholly unconcerned with one another. They rigidly face their allotted melody portions and nothing else; among themselves they are poor neighbors. (The objectionable "consecutive fifths" are irrelevant under the present consideration.)

With the use of the chord-inversions (Ex. 7) this rudeness disappears instantly. The poor neighbors become good neighbors; that is, though still conscious of their primary task, at the same time they obligingly extend their hands, as it were, to their neighbors. *Harmonic* and *chordal* functions meet.

Theory usually attacks this problem by advising that each member of a harmony should take, on principle, the smallest step into membership in the neighboring harmony. While this axiom seems a simple and practical expedient for the beginner, it implants in him a dangerous misconception, namely the viewpoint of the rigidly *preconceived* harmony as a fixed unit, or pattern, within the frame of which each voice seeks to take up its appropriate place.

This narrow view must from the very beginning be replaced by the wider and superior view of the inherent urge of each voice toward linear self-preservation.

It is not enough to know that in the course of musical progression each tone asserts its membership in the harmony in which it is imbedded as well as in the melodic line of which it is part. The truth is that the melodic impulse is primary, and always preponderates over the harmonic; that the melodic, or linear, impulse is the force out of which germinates not only harmony but also counterpoint and form. For the linear impulse is activated by *motion,* and motion means life, creation, propagation and formation.

Just as the moving mists and clouds adopt the most diverse shapes in constant integration, diffusion and re-formation, thus the moving voices in music result in constantly changing harmonies.

To illustrate this point let us harmonize a short phrase like Ex. 8.

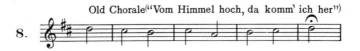

Old Chorale("Vom Himmel hoch, da komm' ich her")

Ex. 9 shows a most common, so to speak academic garden variety of such a harmonization:

There is really nothing wrong with this harmonization. Considering that it has to do with a chorale to be sung by or for a congregation in the church whose devotion it is meant to serve without deflecting their minds into conscious art-considerations, we may perfectly agree to it. However, taking this chorale melody, or just part of it, as a foil for demonstration and study, we will forget about congregation and church and concentrate on our objective of showing how harmony may generate from linear impulses.

Ex. 10-21 show a variety of other harmonizations.

We suggest that the reader play singly first each of the four voices of each example. Next he might play any single voice together with the cantus firmus (the soprano). Only then should he play all four voices together, slowly, abiding for a while on each harmony in order to sense the desire, leaning and tendency of each harmony. Not too many variants should be tried at a time, so that the impressions may have a chance to settle.

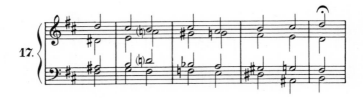

Most of the harmonies as presented in Ex 10-21, if singled out and detached from their context, would prove nondescript in the light of traditional harmony. Everything opposed to it seems to be piled up: consecutive fifths, cross relations, spiteful coincidence of natural and altered steps, occasionally arbitrary dissonances. And yet we hope that the reader, even though these harmonizations may appear unusual and strange to him, will feel their logic and organic life. That they are arrived at by linear voice-leading, is obvious.

The principle of linear writing advocates melodic independence, which involves *movement* of voices. The principle of traditional harmonic writing, by assigning each voice its predetermined place, above all by making it sustain common tones of neighboring harmonies, suppresses melodic independence. It actually enslaves the voices, especially the middle voices, into the unconditional service of the taskmaster, harmony; whereas recognition of their inborn urge to move makes for a healthy democracy among all voices in which harmony thrives as well as melody.

A comparison of each single voice of Ex. 9 with each single voice of Ex. 10-21 will reveal this status. And their ensemble will reveal that the liberation of the voices triumphs over the fixed conception of harmony with all its implications, including its most dreaded shadow, the "dissonance".

Consonance and dissonance

In order to discuss these terms, we must first put aside their popular connotations of "beautiful" and "ugly". The identification of the "dissonance" with "cacophony" or, for that matter, with any aesthetic consideration whatsoever does not touch the technical significance of the term. Nor does the wholesale rejection of contemporary music of any epoch because of its "dissonances" differ in any way from the wholesale rejection of any innovation in any field of art or science before its general acceptance.

It would be hard indeed for us today to imagine that passages like Ex. 22 or 23 should have sounded "ugly" at any time:

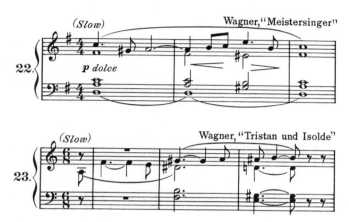

So let us disregard any aesthetic considerations and approach the question from a purely technical viewpoint.

Dissonance can exist only if and where there exists consonance. The two terms are interconditioned as are big and small, light and dark, warm and cold. All these antagonistic concepts which suggest diametrical contrasts, are quite useful indeed as handy communication symbols of our everyday language. In reality, however, the terms of each pair are only different gradations of the same quality, or idea, or phenomenon. Physics does not know warmness and coldness, but just "heat", which covers the whole range from the lowest measurable or conceivable temperature ("degree of heat") to the highest. A certain definite temperature, felt as a chill if suddenly occurring in the tropics, will be felt as real heat in the arctic regions. Man is a huge giant as against the microbe, yet himself a microbe in the face of a glacier.

Between these two arbitrarily selected sizes are innumerable others, filing progressively by in an endless row. In the light of light there are countless shades of shade. At what point does the dark, the small, the cold cease and the light, the big, the warm begin?

No one will deny that the last chords of Ex. 22 and 23 are felt, after the preceding trembling tensions, as soothing and reconciling sounds endowed with all the intrinsic essence of the "consonance". And yet, in the practical everyday language of music these dominant seventh-chords are the prototypes of the dissonance, expected by theory to "resolve" into their respective triads—the prototypes of consonance.

For this is what theory declares: (1) That dissonance does not find repose in itself, and therefore does not satisfy the ear, but needs to "resolve", meaning to be followed by consonance, in which the ear may find repose and satisfaction; and (2) That certain sounds, intervals or harmonies are by nature dissonant, and others are by nature consonant. For instance seventh-chords are dissonant — a kind of black sheep; whereas triads are consonant — white sheep.

According to these fundamentals there can be no doubt left as to which of the two chords, seventh chord and triad, finds repose in itself and which does not; and therefore, which must resolve into which.

The following example (24) exposes a triad at + and a seventh-chord at ⊙.

If we stop playing at +, the want of repose, the urge to "resolve", in short, the dissonance-character of the chord as laid down by theory, is patent. Just as patent is the achieved repose, the hallmark of consonance, in the subsequent seventh chord at ⊙. In fact, so strong is the urge of the dissonant *triad* at + to resolve that it impatiently anticipates by one eighth-note the craved-for resolution — into the *seventh chord*. Black and white sheep have quite naturally and peaceably exchanged their colors.

Here are a few classical quotations:

Beethoven, 5th Symphony

28.

Mahler, 2nd Symphony

29.

(Alto Solo)

O glau-be,   mein Herz,___ o_ glau-be

Reprinted by permission of the copyright owners in the U. S. A.
Boosey & Hawkes, Inc., 668 Fifth Avenue, New York City

Beethoven, 7th Symphony

30.

Weber, "Der Freischütz"

Him - mel, nimm des Dan - kes Zäh - ren

31.

Disregarding chordal inversions, in Ex. 25 triad resolves into seventh-chord; in Ex. 26-31 dissonant triads resolve into consonant triads; in Ex. 25, 30, 31 the third is dissonant, in Ex. 26, 27 the fifth, in Ex. 28, 29 the root; in Ex. 26, 27 the dissonances form suspensions, in Ex. 25, 30, 31 passing tones, in Ex. 28, 29, appoggiaturas. Ex. 30, 31 exhibit quite capricious variants in that each juxtaposes one major and one minor triad, either being alternatively the resolution of the other.

So far it may be concluded beyond any discussion that no sound, considered by itself and detached from any context, can under any circumstances be other than neutral and meaningless, just as no letter of the alphabet can be anything but neutral and meaningless. To divide any kind of sounds, be it tones, intervals or harmonies, into one category of consonances *per se* — white sheep — and another one of dissonances *per se* — black sheep — is as absurd as it would be to divide the letters of the alphabet into consonances and dissonances.

The sooner we discard these two coddled pets of theory, the sooner we will discard with them an unending source of confusion. The future will look back at this doctrine of consonances and dissonances with the same pitying smile which we bestow upon the once-upon-a-time belief in witches and evil demons living inside certain individuals.

In the question of consonance and dissonance physics is not quite innocent in that it puts up the following, generally accepted statement: The simpler the ratio of the vibration-numbers of two tones, the more pleasant or "consonant" is their impression on the ear; the more complicated this ratio, the more unpleasant or "dissonant" is their impression.

This statement contains the following implications:

1. It identifies the terms consonant and pleasant, or dissonant and unpleasant.

2. It attributes the terms to definite, predetermined sounds (intervals in that case), independent of the context in which they appear.

It is not so surprising after all that the physicist or the physicists reponsible for this statement so far adopted the current maxims of the musical experts, since a scientist in one field would not hesitate to use for his own purposes the findings of the accredited authorities in another field. But the physical statement involves two more implications on which physics evidently departs from the theory of music and stands on its own feet, in fact points at qualities which musical theory so far has failed to acknowledge:

3. The statement of physics, in contrast to musical theory does *not* lay down any *absolute concept* of consonance and dissonance, thus suggesting the questionability of their existence as absolute phenomena.

4. It clearly suggests that they too, like warm and cold, etc., may be but different gradations of one quality, idea, or phenomenon.

While we heartily accept and acclaim the second pair of these implications, it requires little effort to refute the first pair.

According to the vibration ratio of the whole diatonic major scale, which is

$$1 : \frac{9}{8} : \frac{5}{4} : \frac{4}{3} : \frac{3}{2} : \frac{5}{3} : \frac{15}{8} : 2$$
$$c \quad\ d \quad\ e \quad\ f \quad\ g \quad\ a \quad\ b \quad c^1$$

the numeral relationship of the octave is the simplest of all, namely 1:2, while the vibration ratio of all the other intervals is represented by fractions. Thus, if among the intervals there should exist any "white sheep" at all, the octave must be the "whitest" of all. Contrasted to the ninth, whose vibration ratio, according to the continued table, would be $1:\frac{9}{.4}$, there can again be no doubt as to which of the two is the consonance, which the dissonance and which the resolution of which.

We need but to reduce Ex. 24 to its outer contours (**Ex. 32**)

to see that this relationship of octave and ninth is flatly reversed. For it is evident that the octave in this case (+) does not find repose in itself, and therefore does not satisfy the ear, but needs to resolve into the subsequent ninth (☉).

Thus it is with intervals as it is with chords: The urge to move onward in one case, and the satisfaction of this urge in another case, is as little inherent in certain predetermined intervals as it is in predetermined chords. These qualities are essentials of the moving voices that meet in intervals or chords.

If we play the voices of Ex. 32 *singly,* the urge to move on manifests itself in either voice as soon as it arrives at the point marked by +. The fact that the voices, at this point, meet in the interval of the octave, is purely accidental and without any consequence. *Any interval at this intersection*

would be bound to be dissonant. Likewise any interval acci-
dentally forming in the consistent course of two voices at
the point of ⊙ would provide the resolution, as can be seen
best by playing any combination of two voices of Ex. 24.

For in the end any sound—tone, interval or chord—once
exposed to the force of attraction which emanates from the
tonic, seeks to reach the tonic (dissolve, "resolve" into it)
either directly or indirectly through the *sphere* of attraction
that surrounds the tonic as its center.

Through this magnetic sphere, which is composed of all
the secondary steps of the key (augmented sometimes by
artfully altered, substituted, borrowed steps) the sound
would gradually drift before finally yielding to the tonic.
(See Ex. 78).

In order to activate this force of attraction, its center,
the tonic—in other words the key—has first to be indubitably
established. The reason why certain sounds in Ex. 24-32 show
dissonance tendencies, in spite of their being consonances in
the traditional sense, is that they are sharply exposed to
their respective spheres of attraction. The reason why the
harmonies of Ex. 39, 40 lack these dissonance tendencies, in
spite of their being dissonances in the traditional sense, is
that no tonic, that is, no center and no sphere of attraction,
is given a chance to establish itself. Again, with the inten-
tional suspension of any such tone center or center of attraction — the style that in our days is called "atonality" — the
consonance-dissonance theory in any sense whatsoever is
bound to collapse, and any attempt to apply its dogma must
meet with perplexity and frustration.

Now this so-called atonality is a last stage of gradual
evolution, a last conclusion drawn from ever present, if not
always equally apparent principles.

The following example:

shows in bar 2, second half, a series of chords which progressively lead back to the key of E flat major. The charm of this progression lies in the fact that for a short stretch the power of attraction of the key-note *eb* is somehow suspended, or dimmed, and gradually reinstituted. We may say that this force is temporarily superseded by a stronger force—motion, momentum, inertia, whatever we may call it—until it asserts itself again and in turn supersedes the intermediate other force. Similarly, the vertically operating force of gravity may sometimes be neutralized by a stronger force effective in horizontal direction. Now if gravity can be neutralized at all, it makes no difference whether a moth flies through a room or an airship flies around the globe. Thus if the attracting force of the tonic can be neutralized at all, it makes no difference whether it is neutralized for no matter how short a passage of a musical piece or for a whole piece — atonality.

To come back now to Ex. 33: Let us for the sake of an illustrating experiment replace the progressions of bar 2 by other progressions as shown for instance in Ex. 34 and 34a.

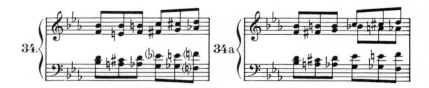

The changes applied to the original are essential only in one point: while Chopin kept the composition within the traditional limits of chords of the third-system, the two variants present some tone-combinations that would defy such classification.

Ideologically, however, there is no difference between the original and the two variants. The musical function of the passage, namely the temporary suspension of the key and its reinstatement after the short episode, is certainly equally patent in all three versions. The preservation of the purity of style which would make such a replacement inconsistent with the rest of the composition must not blind us to the essential validity of the argument in question.

It would be out of place to view these substituted tone-combinations as "chords"; it would be equally out of place to view the original Chopin passage as "modulations" through different keys — with none of such keys established and none of the chords *in office,* though shamming the gown; but most of all, it would be out of place to view the original as containing one consonant chord—the *e* major triad—among dissonant chords, and the two variants as containing only dissonant chords.

The whole consonance-dissonance problem collapses again, its argument being beside the point.

The phases of the passage are not felt and cannot be interpreted as *either consonant or dissonant* but only as co-incidences of voices in motion, each of them propelled horizontally and creating its own momentum, and with it the momentum of the tone-combinations in which they happen to meet.

Thus they expose the real, intrinsic conception of harmony. For although harmony may still be defined as the combination of three or more tones, it has to be interpreted beyond this concept as a momentary situation brought about by moving voices; as the cross-section arising at times of arrested motion; or briefly and plainly as *arrested motion*.

It is the specific, momentary situation in midcourse of motion which endows a harmony with more or less momentum as the case may be; it is the absence of such motion which renders a harmony *per se* neutral.

A moving picture, stopped at a particular moment, may exhibit a group of people violently gesticulating, their faces passionately distorted. A newspaper picture may show a swimmer hovering in mid-air in perfect diving form, the diving board still vibrating from his take-off. A monument may show a rider on horseback, the horse rearing on its hind legs, the rider leaning forward, tightening the reins. We pass the movie scene, used perhaps for advertisement on a poster, time and again, without marveling that the people have not yet calmed down; the newspaper, lying around for any length of time, occasionally catches our eye and we do not marvel that the diver is still suspended in mid-air, the board still vibrating; the equestrian statue may outlive generations without anybody wondering at the strain of the pose. This is because our imagination automatically and empirically furnishes the missing real motion, of which, arrested at particular moments, these exposures are but visible symbols.

For *motion* it is, real or imaginary, that gives sense and meaning to these symbols, as it gives sense and meaning to the audible symbols. The very sentence I am writing now would leave me wondering and unsatisfied if stopped after any of its words except the last. Shall we now solemnly proclaim the word "LAST", — l-a-s-t — a consonance and the rest of those words dissonances, demon-possessed witches? Any word may be the first, the middle or the last of a sentence. And so the mediaeval witch-burners were doubly wrong; first because no girl is a witch and second because all girls are witches.

And as to harmonies — they all are consonances and they all are dissonances; or rather, harmony, consonance and dissonance, they all are the same — the same substance, or phenomenon, or idea — *arrested motion*.

CHAPTER II

HARMONY AS ARRESTED MOTION

In the light of the foregoing considerations, the difference between the notions "harmony" and "chord" clears up and broadens.

While the notion "chord" carries much more the flavor of something solid, static, substantial, measurable; the "harmony" notion implies the aspect of the fluid, unsubstantial, immeasureable. We may say chord is to harmony as body is to soul; or harmony is the soul of the chord. It may suit the chord, the honeycomb frame of combined intervals, to enter classification by measurements and mathematical symbols. If we try to force harmony into such rigid objectivity, it escapes this compulsion by a hundred loopholes.

Even our everyday language senses this difference of meaning — the technical narrowness of the chord-notion as against the trans-technical implications of the harmony-notion. We speak of spheric harmonies but not of spheric chords; and Pythagoras and his followers, innocent of future harmony textbooks with figured bass and the like, were uninhibited in visualizing, or "audializing", these *harmonies* of the spheres. Similarly we speak of eternal harmony, a harmonious person, a harmonious marriage, but not of an eternal chord, a chordal person, a chordal marriage. Behind the corporeal substantiality of the chord hides the sensitive soul of harmony.

It is worthwhile to know about the chords, their structure and consistency and it is commendable for the beginner to learn about them as a kind of foundation and a serviceable basis of communication. But if he stops at this system he will be at the mercy of fatal limitations, inhibitions and perplexities; he will be doomed *not to see the forest for the trees*.

Beware of restraining the harmony phenomenon in a prison of mathematical symbols. It will revolt against such constraint and it will baffle you. If you want to penetrate to its core and disarm it, you must leave your measurements and figures at home and approach it, as it were, unarmed yourself. Heraclitus' basic principle «*Πάντα ῥεῖ*» ("everything is in flux") will serve you better as a sesame to open the door and win to the heart of harmony.

It is from such a vantage point that the infinite expressiveness of the definite "harmony", even in the classical vocabulary, becomes luminous. What seems to recur again and again in the same outer appearance, is in fact a different substance in each different concatenation of events.

The influence of the situation

Do you know about the hydraulic cycle? It is so perfectly closed in itself that no one can tell where it starts. Chemistry calls water H_2O. But this H_2O is given in a continuous chain of situations, each a link between others. The cloud, the rain-drop, drizzle and cloud-burst; the snow-flake and the single snow-crystal, sleet, the hail-stone, and ice; fog and dew; the spring, the brook, the stream, the ocean; vapor and steam — which is the real H_2O? It is liquid, solid and gaseous; it is without color, light-green and dark-blue. Even the rainbow is H_2O under certain conditions, in a certain situation. Put the tone in place of the molecule and you have the multiplicity of its appearances. Put the harmony in place of the drop and you get the multiplicity of its situations. What else is $\frac{5}{3}$ here than H_2O there? Both symbols are serviceable tools for a certain approach. But the one should not be more to the musician than the other is to the painter or the poet. He must be able to entirely forget about them when he approaches the work of art, be it as creator, percipient, or student of harmony.

A few illustrations will show harmony in different situations. In Ex. 35.

the function, or the "situation", of the two fundamental harmonies of the key (tonic and dominant) is such that they simply and obviously give support to the equally simple melody. The composition is so essentially and exclusively rooted in the melody that it would clearly and unmistakably convey its meaning even without the actual sounding of the (by nature quasi) inherent harmonization.

In Ex. 36

the situation is exactly reversed. Here nothing exists to be harmonized at all. The composition rests entirely in the progression of harmonies, as many other works of Bach do. So utterly unessential to the composer seem all events which could possibly be grouped around those harmonies that he leaves them completely to the discretion of the improvising player. To be sure, the art of improvisation in those times

was highly developed but it is difficult to say what was the
cause and what the effect. In other cases of similar order
Bach himself would add such an improvisation, as for instance in the first Prelude of the "Well-tempered Clavichord". The special pattern of broken chords established by
the composer is so familiar to us that we would consider it
a crime to change it. But to Bach's contemporaries it would
have appeared perfectly natural to vary the given pattern of
chord-breaking (Ex. 37) by other patterns such as Ex. 37a
and 37b, as they were accustomed to do in so many other compositions of this type where it was actually left to them.

In the following example

the situation of harmony is about midway between its situations in the two preceding quotations by Schubert and
Bach. Here the musical event is based neither on the bare
melody nor on the bare harmony. Equivalent in measure and
weight, the one dissolves in the other like a tablet in water,
into a homogeneous substance. As support here, almost more
for rhythmical accentuation than actual harmonization, the
sparse touches of the bass are sufficient.

In Ex. 39 and 40

Permission granted by Jean Jobert, Paris, and
Elkan-Vogel Co., Inc., Philadelphia, Pa., copyright owners

chords line up which all show the same interval-structure. The fact that this structure makes each of them a dominant-ninth of some major key seems to be of little import. None of them accepts the consequence of its ninth, of its position on the dominant, or of its membership in any key. Both passages exhibit a chain of ninth-chords none of which even so much as attempts to "resolve" in any way. With the temporary suspension of any established key (just by the very chain of isolated new dominants) the feeling of the dissonance-quality, that is, the urge for resolution of these chords, disappears. They have ceased to possess a causal relation of tonality to each other or to a common tone-center. The relation of tonal causality gives way to the mere sensation of a "sound-impression" *per se*.

Again harmony has entered a new situation. That it still retains — an item of utter unimportance — the outer garment of a chord of the third-system may be attributed to a last residue of conscience in which the composer was steeped by tradition and education. If the chord-pattern were even more dissonant in the traditional sense its effect could (and most probably would) be still softer, still more irridescent, still more "impressionistic". At any rate, in spite of third-structure and compatibility with the old classification, harmony has abandoned entirely its static, objective quality.

In Moussorgsky's "Boris Godunow" (Ex. 41) a long
scene — people praying in front of a church — is illustrated
musically by two constantly alternating harmonies:

Moussorgsky,"Boris Godunow"

To the harmonies are added (apart from changes in orchestration) various patterns of chord-breaking in the high registers of the orchestra such as:

But aside from this—with reference to themes, melodic development, musical flow, etc.—nothing happens. Here also
the two harmonies are dissonant chords of the third-system,
the most simple and the most frequent: dominant seventh
chords expected by tradition to resolve into the tonic some
time. But who now recognizes them as such, who now
would think with the first one of *db* major or minor and

with the second one of *g* major or minor, the only keys to which they belong? They never resolve and no one misses a resolution. They support no melody and no one misses a melody. They establish no key and no one misses a key.

Detached from any harmonic or melodic causality, liberated from the ties of their origin, they are but sounds freely floating around in space, harmony in its aboriginal power and without any other musical consequence, like the sound of church-bells, mighty and primordeal in their effect as we may imagine the "harmony of the spheres". Again the outer garment of their chordal structure and their apparent membership in certain keys is purely accidental. Again it was a last inhibition which, for all the lure and for all the power of his vision, restrained the composer from shaking off the fetters of third-bound theory.

He who in the sparkling tone-glitter of the silver-rose in Strauss' "Rosenkavalier" (Ex. 44, 44a)

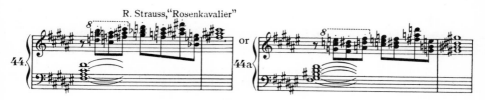

Reprinted by permission of the copyright owners in the U. S. A. Boosey & Hawkes, Inc., 668 Fifth Avenue, New York City

should attempt to refer the sounds to the common denominator of the "figured bass" would soon have to desist. Still, it can hardly be imagined that the lovely and so "false" celeste-chords should ever have hurt anyone's ear. Do they not in their light-refractions and tone-reflections come strikingly near to the "rainbow" situation of the substance H_2O?

Yet with all these manifestations of an impressionistic sound-expression the non-static, fluid character of the harmony-phenomenon is not exhausted. They only represent another outlet among the many through which at different times, with more or less timidity or determination, harmony made its way into the open. Besides, the examples from "Rosenkavalier" need not be evaluated only from the viewpoint of impressionism. They emanate also from another point, the coincidence of different *"streams"*. It would obviously be absurd to relate what goes on in the moving chords of the upper register to the harmonies sustained in the lower register. The latter form a sound-community united by one idea, or one harmonic will; the chord-group fleetingly drifting above it another community, united by another idea, or harmonic will. In this case it happens that the group of sustained harmonies adheres to one tone-center, or key; the group in motion, unattached to any such center, revolves loosely around the first.

The simultaneity of such sound-streams is one of the chief reasons for the repudiation of the conception of harmony as a static object rooted in structural patterns.

At the bottom of a musical phrase like Ex. 45

Bach, Fantasy and Fugue (G Minor)

lies the interminably recurring cadential formula of Ex. 45a. But the voices of the soprano and tenor, moving linearly,

clash in the triple coincidence of the tones *g* and *a,* marked
+, while they struggle to free themselves from the firm grip
of the cadential harmonies. (Note also the *c* in the soprano.)

Only from the viewpoint of linear streams can such
sounds as the ones marked in Ex. 46 be judged at all.

But such sounds in their tame and playfully ornamental
form are hardly noticeable nor are they characteristic of
Beethoven's sometimes provocative recklessness. In Ex. 47
the linear voice-leading takes on a considerably different
appearance.

The shortness of the phrase does not render its conception less linear. Moreover it is written for such a percussive
sound quality as the piano and lies most awkwardly for the
player. This is one of the many instances to show how little
Beethoven cared about an easy technical sleekness and how
exclusively he was concerned with the pursuit of the abstract
idea — in this case the imitation of the motif in stretto.

Likewise unconcernedly he interpenetrates tonic **triad and dominant** seventh-chord in the following stretto:

Beethoven, Sonata Op. 81a

The boldness of this example consists in the concurrence of those four tones embracing the most heterogeneous harmonies, tonic and dominant, so to speak the positive and negative poles. Thus the complete mutual penetration of these polar harmonies flashes up momentarily. The following little phrase contains the same tone-structures (Ex. 49, +):

Where did the boldness vanish all of a sudden? The phrase is not a quotation from an existing classical composition, yet invented so much in the classical idiom that it easily could occur in any such composition. Belonging no longer to two different streams — the polar harmonies of tonic and dominant — the sound-compounds have changed their *situations* completely.

In another passage, famous and much disputed for that reason, Beethoven puts the two polar harmonies directly and unexpectedly into one another:

Beethoven, 3rd Symphony

Theory with its *idée fixe* of the systematized chordal structures, regarding harmony as a solid object, finds itself puzzled and cornered by such unruliness. Anxious, nevertheless, to keep up its dogma, it resorts to excuses and subterfuges, administers "exceptional" privileges, issues special passports and remains stubbornly blind to the fact that the crisis, scantily patched up at one point, is bound to recrudesce unexpectedly at a hundred other points. What is the good of finding terms for all the emerging "non-harmonic" events? Will it really help in the end? Will it strike home? If we acquiesce at the "free anticipation" of Ex. 50, what about Ex. 48, let alone 44 and 44a? Shall we call the *f* in the tenor of Ex. 48, bar 3, a "passing tone"? In point of fact this example alone, written one and a half centuries ago, should suffice to elucidate the whole issue. Moreover, it should suffice to point out, from one viewpoint at least, the constant, inevitable, illimitable evolution of harmony to come.

Solid objects are subject to the law of impermeability; but not sounds. Not being solid objects, they can easily penetrate each other. In Ex. 48 two harmonic streams, we may say two sound beams, penetrate each other as two light beams would do; and the image of their intersections is the image of their motion arrested at those particular moments. As two or more light-beams would produce a certain color at the point of their intersection, unforeseen perhaps, yet easily intelligible as the result of its several color components; similarly, two or more sound-beams produce a certain harmony at the point of their intersection, not preconceived, classified or classifiable, yet intelligible for the ear as the result of its sound components and in no need of any excuse, exceptional privilege or passport.

If we play a scale of sixth-chords in contrary motion as shown in Ex. 51,

the resulting harmonies are sufficiently explained by the two moving streams and we need not bother about their particular appearances, their individual registration and classification. They are bound to produce an intelligible, logical and *pleasant* impression.

Venturing one step further, we may as well combine two such streams which no longer belong to the same key (Ex. 52 and 52a):

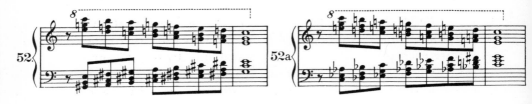

or, in other variants (Ex. 53 and 53a) change the keys midcourse of each stream:

The logic still holds good; the sounds still penetrate each other readily and, if anything, affect us as being still more velvety than if they belonged to the same key. At the same time, they vouchsafe a glimpse into "polytonality" (Ex. 52, 52a) or expose coincidences of "borrowed", or "vicarious" tones (Ex. 53, 53a). These two latter features often overlap, their borderline being hard to define.

Of course, in actual composition independent streams need not and will not appear just in scales; nor need each stream express full harmonies, but they may partly or wholly be reduced to lines. In other words harmonies may combine with harmonies (Ex. 54, 56, 60, 63), or harmonies may combine with lines (Ex. 57, 59, 61), or lines may combine with lines (Ex. 62a).

Here are a few illustrations:

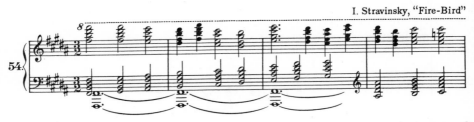

I. Stravinsky, "Fire-Bird"

54.

(monotonal)

Debussy, "Pelleas and Melisande"

55.

(monotonal)

Prokofieff, "Peter and the Wolf"

56.

(polytonal)

Prokofieff, "Sarcasmes," Op. 17 No. 3

57.

(polytonal)

Shostakovich, Prelude Op. 34 No. 9

58.

(polytonal)

Roy Harris, Sonata Op. 7

59.

(polytonal)

ibidem

60.

(streams establishing no key)

Aaron Copland, "Sentimental Melody"

61.

(polytonal or vicarious steps)

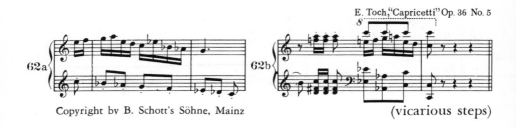

(vicarious steps)

(streams establishing no key)

By vicarious steps we understand altered — more frequently lowered than raised — steps. Their use abundantly prevails in classical music. Here are a few examples.

Ex. 64-66 show the low second step (supertonic) instead of its normal, or authentic form. In Ex. 67-70 the respective authentic and vicarious pitches are playfully juxtaposed:

Still, the actual coincidence, the complete interpenetration of such authentic steps and their vicarious forms, is somehow alien to the classical idiom.

Ex. 71-73 show authentic and vicarious pitches in stringent interpenetration:

Copyright 1935 by Gershwin Publishing Corp. Reprinted by permission.

One needs but to restore equality of the unruly pitches by playing either f or $f\sharp$ in Ex. 71·, and either d or $d\sharp$ in Ex. 72, in both melody and harmony (in short in both hands) to feel the dullness of such attempted "rectification", as against the succulence of the original. The two passages reveal the sure and uninhibited instinct of the composer.

Harmonies are not solid objects.

As has been said, Ex. 48 would suffice to confirm this axiom and point out the direction of the evolution of harmony at least from one angle, the interpenetration of harmonic streams.

CHAPTER III

THE EXPANDING HARMONIC UNIVERSE

In the preceding discussion of interpenetrating harmonic streams, each stream derived its interval structure from the traditional method of superposing thirds (including even passages of such contemporary diction as Ex. 59-63). If we consider, however, that the method of superposing thirds is not the only generating source of harmonies, the harmonic scope widens considerably.

Perfect fourths or fifths, superposed on one another, travel through all our twelve half-tones before returning to the starting point. Thus they form a completely closed circle, which gives them the advantage over the thirds of incomparably greater variety for harmonic building material. As to tonality, a series of seven perfect fourths or fifths still belong to one major key, embracing all its seven steps.

Ex. 74a, b show such fourth-harmonies in monotonality (a) and polytonality (b).

If we further consider that these intervals can also be altered (augmented fourth, diminished fifth) and harmonies may contain both perfect and altered forms of fourths or fifths, the harmonic scope again widens considerably.

Ex. 75 shows a motif employing such harmonies.

Besides, we must also remember that our diatonic major and minor scales are not the only possible ones to be taken as bases for composition. Many other scales, containing seven steps or more or less, have been constructed and used by some composers, e.g. Slonimsky, Tscherepnine, and Holst. Nor need the row of our twelve half-steps be confined to the space of one octave, but may be parcelled out within a two-octave space, omitting the first perfect octave or any other repetition of pitch. It is evident that by such practice again the harmonic scope is bound to widen. There is also, of course, the whole-tone scale.

True, should all these leads be followed up exhaustively, one would arrive at intersecting results occasionally and certain sound-combinations would appear as simultaneously belonging to different systems. Even so, measured against the vast array of harmonic combinations that these considerations are bound to afford, must not the few miserable chords tabulated by traditional theory appear as a pitifully poor stock?

How proudly do we display certain findings like the "Neapolitan sixth" or the "augmented sixth"! Is not one passage like Ex. 64 enough to reveal the former's true nature, sixth or no sixth? Does it not evidence the full citizenship of the low supertonic in the key — root-position or inversion? And do not the subsequent examples up to Ex. 73 exhibit the whole argument — the *exchangeability of low and high steps* — in a nutshell? We certainly would not interpret bars 2 and 6 of Ex. 69 as composed in the key of *c* minor, in the midst of a lengthy *c* major passage. Nor did the composer of Ex. 70 mean to change the *key* in bars 2 and 5.

The activating cause of these two passages is rather to be found in their *melodies* which employ both the low and high forms of one step alternately and thus occasion an incidental change of harmony.

It happens at times that some authentic member of the key, altered into its substitute, appears *by chance* imbedded in a harmony which is still simple and familiar to us by old acquaintance, a specimen of the third system. The altered step in such a case remains inconspicuous and we accept the substituted harmony without further ado; in fact its disguise makes us apt to misinterpret its true nature by taking for a harmonic event what in reality is a sheer melodic event. Such is the case in Ex. 69, 70 (cf. also Ex. 30, 31).

At other times, however, it happens that such an alteration produces a harmony which, *by chance again,* no longer coincides in appearance with a familiar one but makes the altered step somehow protrude conspicuously beyond the familiar chordal frame. Such is the case in Ex. 67.

The promoting idea in Ex. 67, 68 and 69 is always the same: the playful alternation of an authentic and its vicarious step as a *sheer melodic event.*

In Ex. 69 this altered step happens to be the third; in
Ex. 67 and 68 the supertonic, the "Neapolitan" pitch. In
Ex. 68 the playful turn of the melody lies in the upper voice,
in Ex. 67 it happens to lie in the bass.

Inconspicuous harmonically in its authentic form, (Ex.
76, at +), it instantly becomes harmonically conspicuous in

its altered form (⊙). And instantly we pounce upon it, **tag
and needle drawn, and pin the label on it. A new harmony
has been discovered, hallelujah! Triumphantly we parade it,
put it in a shrine and worship it. The collection of chords
has been increased by one. Now the student of harmony, if
he wants to cover all of it, has to add to his knowledge of
triads, seventh-chords, ninth-chords and their possible inversions** not only the Neapolitan sixth, but also the *"augmented"* sixth. Does that not sound like a student of botany
flaunting his complete knowledge of the vegetable kingdom
by enumerating exhaustively the oak, the buttercup, the
string bean, the daisy and the walnut?

We are surrounded by an ocean of plants. But we are
indeed surrounded by an ocean of harmonies as well. Why
do we shut our eyes to this fact? Is it because we shrink
from the Gargantuan task of labelling them all, and from the
super-Gargantuan task of committing them to memory?
There is an easy way out: Stop attempting to label them by
measures and symbols. Stop regimenting them as though they
were solid objects. Give up the stubborn, unfruitful view of

the static and adopt the more productive view of the instantaneous image of an ever fluid, ever-fluctuating, ever-gyrating phenomenon; the view of the ever changing relation of a stellar body to the rest of the universe, the view of the Heraclitean axiom, "Everything is in flux."

Subdivision of the half-tone

All these investigations were based on our system of twelve half-tones, the product of the subdivision of the perfect octave into twelve tolerably equal tone-spaces. This subdivision is by no means an irrefragable, God-given or nature-given fact. Rather we know it to be agreed upon by convention based on artistic — musical — as well as scientific — physical — considerations. Who tells us that this subdivision is the only feasible one? In fact we know that between these half-tones lie an infinite number of other pitches. Moreover, this fact is known to us not only theoretically, but by real and frequent physical experience, strange as it may seem, and in spite of our being unheedful of it.

How particular is a conductor about his orchestra being in perfect tune before starting to play! And how particular is he about having his men play all the pitches as pure and clean as possible! (And justly so!) Yet he does not mind in the least — nor does the audience — hearing the purest harmony blurred, muddled up, in fact all but wiped out, by the collateral roll of a snare drum, the crash of a cymbal, the beat of the bass drum, the gong or the tamtam, the peal of chimes or the mere tinkling of the triangle. Where does his — and our — harmonic conscience vanish all of a sudden?

True, we accept these sounds as incidental and somehow detached from the harmonic events. Yet we cannot deny that their complex sounds contain, beside their material characteristics, numerous nondescript interjacent pitches which could be sifted and bared by acoustical instruments.

A violinist may tune his instrument first to the pitch of one piano and next to the pitch of another piano, perhaps considerably different from the first. Along with the four strings, the whole tonal system, with all the overtones and all the slumbering harmonies, will change by a quarter-tone, more or less.

Suppose someone sings a passage of some length and intricacy, unaccompanied. At the end of it the pitch may show quite a perceptible drop, though the infinitesimal phases of gradual dropping may be hardly discernible. Nor will it actually hurt the ear; and if some musicians make a great fuss over the shortcoming, it will be rather for reasons of professional ostentation than of actual pain. Putting aside all prejudices of training and education, we must admit that the passage as sung by the culprit represents a modulation from one key into another. And if smoothness, evenness, gradualness and imperceptibility constitute professional virtues of such a transition, we·must further admit that no school-modulation can rival this accidental one in these qualities.

What happened? The singer started in one key "X" and finished in another key "Y", say one half tone or so lower. He arrived at this somewhat remote key (remote in the sense of key-relationship) not by way of "legitimate" modulation but by smooth and gradual gliding throughout the passage, as indicated by the diagonal in the diagram (Ex. 77).

77.

On his way he necessarily touched upon a number of other interjacent keys (indicated in the diagram by parallel horizontal lines) or at least used some of their inherent pitches. If he should try to produce this "modulation" intentionally, self-consciousness would probably prevent him from succeeding. The smoothness would be gone.

Does not the idea offer itself to utilize such accidents, to elevate them from the level of casualness to the level of planned organization?

The idea of splitting the half-tone space is old. Since the advent of this century a number of technicians as well as composers have engaged themselves in the production and utilization of sub-halftones (Stein, Möllendorf, Mager, Wishnegradsky, Theremin, Ives, Bartók and above all the Czech composer Alois Hába). During the International Music Festival at Frankfort on Main in 1927 I attended a lecture of Hába on the subject in which he sang for exemplification a chromatic row of quarter-tones and sixth-tones, testing every second quarter-tone or every third sixth-tone by the coinciding chromatic half-tone on the piano. Not only were the pitches distinctly discernible but the ear became used to them quickly, and their scales soon took on an effect equivalent to that of our familiar chromatic scale.

Though such experiments and speculations have no direct bearing on the elemental gift of creative genius, their preparatory value for future music is patent and undeniable. After all it was the tempered system of our twelve tones, arrived at by experiments as well, into which the composers of the past cast their ideas, lighting upon this system through the accidental date of their birth; as poets would use the language into which they were born by accident of date and place.

Speculative as such an approach to quarter-tone music appears, and cryptic as its sound is bound to remain as long as it is not heard and practised generally, it still is not mere technical experiments or academic reflections that point to the use of quarter-tones or otherwise subdivided half-tones. Again it is classical music itself which suggests harmonic evolution in this direction; which, in fact, actually raps at the very gates of sub-halftone music.

In Ex. 78 (somewhat simplified for easier reading or

Brahms, Clarinet-Quintet Op. 115

playing) the three chords which perform the modulation back to b major (⊢———⊣) obviously owe their origin to the linear movement of the three lower voices against the sustained upper voice. The plastic effect of these moving voices, pointed up by the composer through the added dynamics (⊂ ⊃), manifests itself easily to the ear and can be perceived still better if the voices are played singly, one after the other.

The *c* in the cello at the downbeat of bar 7 has a double function. First it continues the preceding upbeat, still supporting the vicarious, Neapolitan-fashioned *c* major triad. But presently it assumes the import and function of a *b*♯, preparing for and leading into the subsequent *c*♯.

The double spelling of the pitch in Ex. 79a is intended to make this change of meaning more evident.

Were the meaning of *c*♮ to prevail throughout the bar, its tendency either to stay in the key or to move downward as shown in Ex. 79b, would suggest itself; contrariwise the interpretation of an obtaining *b*♯ would suggest its growing out of the lower step *b*♮, as shown in Ex. 79c.

The sensitive string player (or singer) will in such cases instinctively adjust the pitch to the tendencies of the particular context. He will take the same pitch higher for example if it represents the "leading-tone" than if it represents the seventh in a dominant seventh-chord, thus increasing the magnetic tension by increased approximation to the goal tone.

Consequently, if the cellist wants to do justice to the

changing meaning of the *c* in this passage, as shown in Ex. 79a, he would have to actualize this change by raising the pitch of the leading-tone-like *b♯* above the pitch of the *c* — the fusion of these two pitches into one being but a compromise of the "tempered" system.

The final solution offers itself with compelling logic. It is shown in Ex. 79d, introducing the quarter-tone above the *c,* as indicated by the arrow pointing upwards. (The arrow pointing downwards is suggested for the quarter-tone below, as applied in Ex. 80b).

Needless to say, this experiment is not meant to "correct" the composition but to demonstrate the issue in question.

It may be objected, however, that the introduction of the eighth-notes in bar 7 somehow disturbs the rhythmical evenness of the modulatory passage. It seems indeed very likely that the composer's concern was to bring about the modulation by equally moving voices, adjusting the motion of the two lowest voices rhythmically to the motion of the second violin which obviously holds the lead in this passage. Starting from a *c* major triad, however, the two lowest voices had no way of moving by steps. The alternative for them would be either to be sustained over the bar-line and wait for their release after the downbeat (Ex. 80a) or to move

within their own harmonic organism. Preferring any kind of motion to stagnation, the composer chose the latter way (Ex. 78), thereby gaining at least the amenity of the "encircling approach" (see page 118) in the viola part.

Only the use of quarter-tones could have satisfied both desirabilities—the preservation of the two harmonic corner-pillars and their linking by even, stepwise convergence in the several voices over the middle chord (Ex. 80b). Or the encircling turn of the viola part could also be retained if so desired (Ex. 80c or 80d).

Ex. 81 shows a similar condition.

Throughout the whole phrase an even rhythm of quarter-notes is maintained in the accompaniment, carried chiefly by the bass. Occasionally the melodic flow of this voice produces unpreconceived harmonies by its linear passage (middle of bars 2 and 6).

Around the advent of the last bar, however, this smooth

rhythmical flow of the bass is balked for three beats, there being no more moving space left for the descending voice. Similarly to Ex. 78 the middle voices take over the maintenance of the rhythm by shifting inside the harmonic organism. And similarly to Ex. 78 the problem could be solved by the use of quarter-tones as shown in Ex. 82a.

Also, the middle voices could be retained, sharing now the rhythmical responsibility and at the same time enriching the harmony (Ex. 82b).

It is recommended that this quarter-tone passage of the bass be sung, while playing the rest of the voices on the piano. One will be surprised at the facility of the task, its novelty being sufficiently eased by its tangible logic.

Whether or not the composers of Ex. 78 and 81 would have chosen to use quarter-tones, presuming their availability at those times, is of no interest. The point is that their practicability is sufficiently proved to make them eligible for use at whatever time.

We need not actually hear the quarter-tone harmonies of Ex. 80 and 82 in order to be sure of their musical logic. For we know they originate with the same logic as for instance the likewise linearly derived harmonies in Ex. 10-21 and therefore must be intelligible, logical and "beautiful".

Furthermore we have come to understand that no harmony *per se,* and therefore none of these quarter-tone harmonies *per se* either, can be anything but neutral and that here again it is their derivation and placement which renders them intelligible, logical and "beautiful".

At one time, it was just the augmented sixth which ventured forth timidly or boldly, as we may view it; and though propelled by a merely melodic impulse and innocent of any harmonic plot, it was pinned down as an isolated, solitary freak of harmony. Yet the hiding-place from which it escaped, this same melodic propulsion, proved and keeps proving an inexhaustible cornucopia of such freaks. The harmonies of Ex. 10-21 as well as the quarter-tone harmonies of Ex. 80 and 82 are nothing else. (Incidentally, the quarter-tone step in Ex. 82b makes the augmented sixth an augmented augmented sixth, which could be further augmented by simultaneously raising the a♯ to its higher quarter-tone.)

Naturally, the eventual introduction of quarter-tones means no displacement of the old chromatic twelve-tone scale but merely its amplification. In the same way and measure as the twelve tones permit the melodic and harmonic use of both diatonic and chromatic pitches, the twenty-four tones still leave at the discretion of the composer the choice, melodically or harmonically, of any diatonic, semi-tonal or quarter-tonal system and any arbitrary mixture of them. We may compose completely atonal music with the twelve half-tones and completely tonal music with twenty-four (or more) sub-halftones, as we have seen in Ex. 80 and 82.

Moreover, we must beware of linking any kind of existing art-material with any kind of personal style, approach or conception of the artist.

The juxtaposition of the two following excerpts (Ex. 83, 84) may throw some light on this subject.

83.

Slow, ♩ = 56

A. Schönberg "Pierrot Lunaire," Op. 21

Flute

Clarinet in A

Violin

'Cello

Reciting Voice

Piano

84.

Ex. 83, though still confined to the twelve half-tones, is far the more radical of the two. It reveals the last consequences of linear writing, in its fine-pencilled fabric producing a harmonic-melodic web of prismatic tenuity.

Ex. 84 on the other hand, in spite of the drastic innovation of the quarter-tones, is, rather, suggestive of the classical style of quartet writing somewhere in the neighborhood of, say, Schumann, with the first violin holding the lead and the three lower voices subdued almost to the task of harmonization, though the tone-material of such harmonization be ever so amplified.

Common to both, however, is the fact that each defies any attempt at a harmonic analysis in the old sense and that both afford a glimpse into the vastness of harmonic variety.

Nor need we, speaking of this vastness, be vague about its numerical realities. In passing, it might well be worthwhile to take a more precise account of such harmonic possibilities.

If we take any four-pitched harmony such as one of our common and familiar seventh-chords, and subject the four pitches to alterations by half-tones or quarter-tones, the number of combinations without repetitions is 625 (namely m^n if n represents the number of the chord-members and m the number of their five appearances — original, raised by half-tone, raised by quarter-tone, lowered by half-tone, lowered by quarter-tone). Ex. 80b shows one of these 625 possible varieties of the original, with its root raised and its fifth lowered both by quarter-tones.

A six part fourth-harmony such as contained in Ex. 74a or b would yield 15625 varieties without repetition.

In the perfect-fourth harmony continued to its end (over five octaves) or the perfect-fifth harmony continued to its end (over seven octaves) we would have to renounce all the alterations by half-tones, for since these harmonies embrace in their anatomy all the 12 tones of our chromatic scale, any half-tone alteration of one of their members would mean the repetition of its chromatic neighbor. Thus *m* in this case is reduced from 5 to 3, (original, raised by quarter-tone, lowered by quarter-tone,) and the resulting number of combinations of such a chord is *only* 531441.

If we disregard quarter-tones entirely and confine ourselves to our system of twelve tempered half-tones, the composer still has at his disposal 4017 different harmonies from three to twelve tones, whereby only the actual pitches are counted regardless of their spelling, their arrangement by intervals or position, in short anything pertaining to chordal structure.

But with all this knowledge we must never lose sight of the more important fact that harmony itself, of three pitches or whatever number, of half-tone or whatever extended system, is but the casual, incidental image of arrested motion, of ever-fluctuating situation, ever-changing meaning and effect.

Looking at what has been achieved in the development of musical material so far, let us enjoy the thought that only a tiny portion of the soil has been tilled as yet, and that by far the major part of work and harvest still lies ahead of us, including that focus of eternal lure and fascination — harmony.

MELODY

Das höchste ist die Gunst, womit der Himmel schaltet,
Das nächste ist die Kunst, womit der Gärtner waltet.

Fr. Rückert, *"Die Weisheit des Brahmanen"*

CHAPTER IV

MELODY VERSUS HARMONY

Would an attempt to treat of melody in a technical way be a presumption? Melody — the very essence of "divine inspiration", bestowed upon chosen master-minds by the grace of God, the most intimate utterance of musical genius, prompted directly by "the voices of angels, the chant of the birds, the murmur of the purling brook or the spell of the silvery moonlight"?

Such conceptions seem to account for the strange fact that so much is being written, taught and studied about harmony and so little, if anything at all, about melody.*

Certainly melody is a matter of inspiration. But so, no less and no more, is harmony. Or are we to assume that Wagner's "Tristan and Isolde", this richest mine of harmonic beauty and novelty, was the fruit of the composer's particular industry in the study of harmony? Nor is counterpoint, nor is form, nor is any artistic skill in any artistic field detachable from inspiration. The one is nothing without the other; both have to meet and to work together.

---

* The author's first ideas on this subject were laid down in his "Beiträge zur Stilkunde der Melodie" (University of Heidelberg, 1921) and later on in his "Melodielehre" (Max Hesse's Verlag, Berlin 1923).

Nature, intuition, inspiration are one thing; analysis, study, skill are another thing. From time immemorial the human mind has tried to hitch both to the star of human progress.

The diamond, as presented by nature, would elicit little enchantment. It takes the highest skill of the cutter, practiced, cultivated and improved through many generations, to make it the coveted jewel. At the same time this accomplished art of the cutter would be a pitiful waste, utterly lost and ineffectual, without nature's gift of the raw diamond.

Every composer knows, and many sketches of the masters give ample proof, that there is a long and hard road from the first inspiration to its final form. And since this applies to melody in the same degree as to harmony and all the rest of the craft, it certainly must appear worthwhile to undertake an analysis of melody, to hearken to the possible forces at work in melody, as in the other musical phenomena, and to make the knowledge of them responsive to the technique of composition.

*   *   *

Melody, though closely interlinked with harmony, differs from it in two fundamental points.

1. While harmony is marked by the temporal *coincidence* of different pitches, melody is marked by their temporal *succession*.

2. While harmony, being a momentary situation, is completely detached from any rhythmical events, such rhythmical events represent a basic and most vital component of melody.

In a harmony the arrangement of the coinciding pitches (interval structure) is irrelevant. A change of their order does *not* change the harmony, as shown in Ex. 3; it has no bearing on the harmony. With the temporal *succession* of pitches, however — the mark of melody — their order becomes most essential. A change of this order changes the melody considerably, as revealed in Ex. 85 to 88.

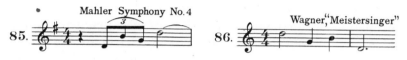

Copyright Boosey & Hawkes, Inc., (U.S.A.)

To be sure, in these four quotations the differences of the rhythmical events play a most vital part, as pointed out above under (2). Yet, disregarding these rhythmical events, the four motifs start with the same four tones, each time in a different order. If we replace their temporal succession by temporal coincidence, the variances vanish and the four melodic individualities concur in one harmonic identity:

Needless to say, the four tones harbor many, many more melodies.

From Ex. 85-88 we learn that a melodic line does not necessarily involve a change in harmony. It is obvious, however, that any change of harmony *necessarily* involves the formation of a melodic line, no matter how short, in the voice or the voices which cause the harmonic change. This subject was extensively discussed in the preceding chapter on harmony, where it was revealed that the melodic progression of one or more voices of a harmony is conducive to the formation, we may say the creation, of ever new harmonies. Melodies, by combination, *integrate* into harmony. Ex. 85-88 show that the frame of a harmony is conducive to the formation, or creation, of ever new melodies. Harmony, by dissolution, *disintegrates* into melody. The two phenomena, melody and harmony, are linked, not closely, but inextricably together.

But short as our Ex. 85-88 are, they teach us much more.

Among the four equal tones of the several motifs* one of them (the tone *d*) appears, or let us cautiously say seems to appear, twice. This duplication is compulsory. For a motif composed solely of the constituents of a triad, which means *three* different tones, and yet embracing *four* tones in its melodic frame, has of necessity to repeat one of them. Yet this is a repetition only in a harmonic sense. In a melodic sense it is *not* a repetition; for melodically speaking the two *d*s are not the same.

While it is correct to say that the twelve tones of our chromatic scale exhaustively present the material of all their harmonic potentialities, it is not correct to say that they exhaustively present the material of all melodic potentialities

---

* The motif of Ex. 87 embraces *five* tones, the (real) repetition of the *g* in its second bar being one of its most essential formative elements. This item will be dealt with separately (page 120ff).

as well. We may acknowledge the multifariousness of harmonies drawn from the twelve tones of an octave; but **we** succumb to a grave fallacy if we apply the same **consideration** to melody — even setting aside all considerations **of** variety in interval successions or rhythmical events.

To begin with, the "twelve tones of an octave" do not embrace an octave but only a major seventh; the octave is the thirteenth tone and as such already a "repetition" of the first. And though it is entirely irrelevant *harmonically* whether we deal with any tone or with its higher or lower octave, it makes all the difference *melodically*.

If we replace the last tone of Ex. 86 by its higher octave, as shown in Ex. 89,

we do not even touch its harmonic frame. That remains exactly the same. But we distort the melody to irrecognizability. A painter might as well curve a line of a profile downward instead of upward and claim no change was made.

This is what would happen (Ex. 90a, b) to another Wagnerian theme (Ex. 91) if we squeeze its expressive gesture into the Procrustean bed of its harmonic frame:

And with horror we may imagine the same procedure
applied to another theme (Ex. 92):

92.   Mendelssohn, Octetto Op. 20

In short, it is nonsense to marvel at the profusion of
melodies that can be drawn from the "seven tones" of a scale,
or the "three tones" of a triad, or the twelve tones available
altogether. To equalize corresponding tones of different octaves, like d, d', d", d'" etc., in a melodic sense is as non-
sensical as it would be to equalize the numbers 2,12,22,32 etc.
From the melodic viewpoint the tone-gamut is unlimited,
though only a limited discernible sector is in practical use,
like the spectrum between the infrared and ultraviolet extremes. It is unlimited like the series of numbers, though,
like this, it renews itself in periodic recurrence, the columns
of tens in mathematics corresponding to the columns of octaves in music. But the melodic line, composed of the various
absolute pitches (absolute according to their real vibration
numbers) is not concerned with the fact that by mere accident, and solely for practical purposes, a certain periodic
recurrence of names was agreed upon, just a such a recurrence of names was agreed upon in the series of numbers.
We could just as well have given each number and each
pitch a name of its own, except that this way things would
have been harder to learn and to remember. Regardless of

any names whatsoever for its single constituents, it is the pitch-line, its curve or curves, its shape, its profile, its ascensions and descensions which determine the character, the *gesture* of the melody — the challenge of Ex. 91, the tenderness of Ex. 86, the exuberance of Ex. 92.

Richard Strauss, in his "Symphonia domestica", draws the last consequence of this consideration by entrusting the violins with a note which is even below the range of the instrument and therefore cannot be produced (Ex. 93).

93.

R. Strauss,"Symphonia Domestica"

Copyright by Bote & Bock, Berlin.
Reprinted by permission of Bote & Bock and Associated Music Publ. Inc.

The passage is reinforced by violas and horns and its sounding thus assured. It would be intolerable, even to the composer's *eye,* to replace the low *f♯* by its higher octave. He wants the line at least to be understood — *playable or not.* And so little does the composer trouble about its impracticibility that he does not even waste a syllable of explanation, perhaps leaving some readers puzzled at the ostensible "blunder".

The different melodic effect of a tone, or a series of tones, in a lower or higher octave becomes especially manifest and attractive when both versions are juxtaposed within an otherwise unchanged phrase (Ex. 94-96) :

(See also Ex. 298)

The adherence to either octave both times would completely destroy the very essence of the musical idea. Ex. 94
would lose the grave dignity of its announcement; the roguish
turn of Ex. 95 would give way to a sodden dullness; while
a dry repetition of the phrase in Ex. 96 would extinguish the
charm of the melody, gracefully soaring away.

The two components of melody

It was said before that any temporal succession of pitches
creates a melodic line, as contrasted with the temporal coincidence of pitches — harmony. It was further mentioned that
there is a second point of contrast between melody and harmony, namely the rhythmic events which are completely
irrelevant to the formation of harmony, yet most vital to the
formation of melody.

In Ex. 97 we perceive such a melodic line, or pitch-line.

97.

Yet it tells us little in the way of a real "melody". We would neither recognize nor enjoy it as such. We do both, however, as soon as the second component of melody, the rhythm, is added:

Beethoven, Violin-Sonata Op. 24

98.

Instantly the lifeless and shapeless frame takes on life and shape, and *beauty*.

The mere pitch-line was a dead wax figure. Rhythm brought it to life. Rhythm became its breath, its soul.

Thus we may roughly define melody as a definite succession of various pitches in a definite succession of rhythms. Such a rough technical definition will serve us for the present in the separate investigation of these two vital components of melody. Beyond this definition, however, and beyond this investigation which we are about to undertake, we must never lose sight of the fact that melody, like everything else under the sun, is much more than its analysis. We know we cannot exhaustively represent the nature of a tree by declaring it the sum of bark, branches, leaves and what not. The more we enjoy our power of improvement by tech-

nical knowledge, the deeper becomes our awareness of the
mystery of origin both in nature and in art, our awareness
of the unanswerableness of the ultimate questions.

If Ex. 97 showed that it is difficult to recognize a melody
by the mere pitch-line divested of rhythm, Ex. 99-101 reveal
that it is less difficult to recognize a melody by the mere
rhythms divested of the pitch-line.

The notation of the pitches *instead* of their rhythmical
patterns, as in Ex. 97, would certainly render Ex. 99-101 less
suggestive of Beethoven's Fifth Symphony, Beethoven's Eg-
mont Overture and Tchaikowsky's Fifth Symphony, respectively.

The rhythmical pattern is the actual backbone of the
motif; it forms the real tie in the motivic structure and makes
itself felt irrespective of tonal changes, be it in imitating
voices (Ex. 102, 103)

or in the continuation of the line, as shown in Ex. 104, 105:

and later:

or, by an amazing coincidence*:

and later

* For the other item which links these two tunes so strikingly together we again refer to page 120ff.

Who on the other hand — to propose a counter-proof —
would ever think of acknowledging any relationship between
Ex. 106 and Ex. 107, though no less than the first ten tones
of the pitch-line show complete conformity?

Following such observations, rhythmical patterns and
pitch-line may be alternately substituted in a continuous
chain. This practice need not and should not be confined to
a game, but will prove a valuable training for the student of
composition. He may start with a known theme, retain the
tonal pattern while changing the rhythm, then retain the
rhythmical pattern with a different pitchline and so forth.
Or he may cast at random a tonal or rhythmical pattern as
he would cast dice and start from there, alternately changing and retaining rhythm and pitch-line, respectively. Sometimes also known melodies may fit as intervening links of
the chain. For example:

Retaining pitch-line, changing rhythm:

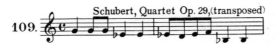

Retaining rhythm, changing pitches:

Same pitches, differently rhythmicized:

Same rhythm with different pitches:

Same pitch-line with different rhythms:

and so forth.

The individual metamorphoses from Ex. 108 to 113 show how the student can make the original motif travel through different styles and, in doing so, can draw a variety of inspirations.

Having divided melody into its two chief components, we will now give its first component, the pitch-line, a closer examination.

The simplest line is the straight line. A horizontal straight line would mean a melody which does not deviate from one pitch but keeps repeating this pitch, at least for a while. To compensate for the lack of tonal variety in such a case, other features would have to be added: varying rhythms, varying harmonies.

In Ex. 114 and 115 the melody repeats its pitch twelve times before leaving it.

The theme of Ex. 116 repeats its first tone no less than

thirty-four times before leaving it.

To be sure, the change of harmonies causes of necessity collateral melodic lines in the middle voices, so that the "line" of the upper voice makes itself felt only when it breaks its monotonous chant in bar 8. Yet, should we ascribe to this upper voice a merely harmonic function, we need but to leave it out (for this harmonic function is sufficiently performed in the *eb* of the lower octave) to see the injustice done to the composer's idea.

A straight line rising or falling at an angle to the horizontal would produce an ascending or descending scale.

Ex. 117 shows such a scale starting on the dominant of the key and carried through one and a half octaves.

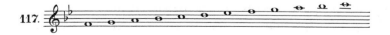

The "melody" looks somewhat problematical. We know what it needs: the help of its other half, the rhythm. This added, we greet an old friend:

Here are a few more illustrations:

In Ex. 121 the even flow of the line appears interrupted, "notched" as it were, at points where the will of the under-lying *harmony* breaks through and makes the harmonical skeleton visible. We will frequently encounter such a contest of forces which results in the partial deflection of each of them, allowing none of them to assert itself unbrokenly.

The pattern of the descending scale shows in Ex. 122, 123:

122. Ca-ro no-me che il mio cor fe-sti pri-mo pal - pi - tar

CHAPTER V

THE WAVE LINE

With the combination of ascending and descending scale-segments melody approaches its real nature: the *wave line* (Ex. 124-127).

The concept of the wave line taken in a wider sense will reveal the line's most frequent shape with it's "ups and downs" not confined to stepwise motion but showing a variety of intervals (Ex. 128-132).

Permission granted by Jean Jobert, Paris, and
Elkan-Vogel Co., Inc., Philadelphia, Pa., copyright owners

It is at this point that a few principles appear to manifest themselves as more or less general and natural maxims among what to the fleeting glance may appear as arbitrary, haphazard melodical events.

If a melody is given time to develop on a broader basis, it shows that the smaller partial waves which constitute the whole line have the tendency to drive upwards their several highest tones (climaxes) until, after reaching the highest of these climaxes, the wave "breaks". The successive climaxes add up, as it were, to one big wave, as marked by **the dotted** line in the diagram.

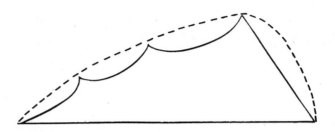

The climax of the last partial wave is at the same time the climax of the melody. Ex. 133 and 134 illustrate these observations.

About the climax of a melody we may say, *in general*:
The climax appears only once.

Its natural place is towards the end of the line, perhaps
in its last quarter or third.

If the melody, in the course of its line, approaches the
pitch of its last climax, it will either not reach this pitch, or
surpass it. Climaxes are exposed tones, and as such, tender
spots. We are sensitive to their repeated exposure. The ear
reacts to the exposure to sound as a photographic film reacts
to the exposure to light. An overdose of such an exposure has
in both cases a blurring effect on the sharpness of the line's
contour.

In order to demonstrate this point we will make a little
experiment with Ex. 133 by replacing one of its progressively rising climaxes by the repetition of another. (Ex. 135,
136, 137).

We feel the unsatisfactory effect of such distorted versions almost to the point of pain. The only possibility to
produce an effect which, though not reaching that of the
original, would still be tolerably satisfactory, would be to
avoid interfering at all with the sensitive pitch by decisively
avoiding its register, as shown in Ex. 138, 139.

It seems as though these characteristics of the melodic line — the single appearance of the climax, and its location near the end, between a long ascending and a short descending branch — would have their roots outside of music or art altogether in physical and psychical provinces.

In the progress of many natural phenomena similar conditions prevail. There are thunderstorms with a marked tendency to rise to mounting fury by comparatively slow degrees and to abate quickly after their most vehement outbursts. It is the pattern of many illnesses to develop slowly towards a "crisis", after which recession and reaction set in quickly. It is also the trend of slowly developing anxieties, fears and hopes to be quickly released after the materialization of their objectives. Finally, the phenomenon touches upon the physical-psychical borderland of our love-life.

These natural tendencies lie, metaphorically speaking, hidden in the work of art. The artist, in the process of creating his work, is not conscious of them. But his work is pulsation and manifestation of nature. Imbuing him, the man, nature imbues his work with her own features.

As the principle functions on a small scale in a defined melody — the germ of form — it functions as a formative element in a whole composition, as will be shown later in the treatment of Form.

Here are a few more illustrations, among which especially the long wide-curved lines of Ex. 140 and 143 foreshadow the influence on form of the above described qualities of a climax.

Reprinted by permission of the copyright owners in the U. S. A.
Boosey & Hawkes, Inc., 668 Fifth Avenue, New York City

Copyright 1946 by Leeds Music Corp., New York, N. Y.

Copyright by B. Schott's Söhne, Mainz
Reprinted by permission of B. Schott's Söhne and Associated Music Pub. Inc.

It must be stressed that the tracing of such a principle
is far from stating a law and far from attempting to cover
the entire field. Its significance is the significance of any attempt at organization and order to the human mind. On
principle, mammals live on solid ground; birds fly; fishes reproduce by spawning. Yet there are mammals which live in
water, birds which do not fly, fishes which give birth to live
young. These facts do not invalidate the principle. It holds
good, no matter how frequently or how rarely it is contro-
verted.

In merely apparent contradiction to the single appearance of the climax are cases where not only the exposed high
pitch appears twice or three times but with it the whole
phrase which includes it. In such instances the repetition of
the climaxing phrase is an intended and well considered
means to increase the rhetorical effect, as an orator would
repeat a whole sentence to which he wishes to give special
emphasis (Ex. 146-148).

klopft   mein   lie - be - vol - les   Herz,   mein   lie - be - vol - les

Herz,   mein   lie - be-vol - les   Herz.

Melodic elasticity

If we subject the small partial waves of the big wave line to a closer examination, we observe that the changes of direction do not occur at random, but favor a certain tendency which may be expressed as follows:

A series of small steps in one direction is, *in general,* followed by a leap in the opposite direction.

Contrariwise, a leap in one direction is, *in general,* followed by a series of small steps in the opposite direction.

We may liken this characteristic to the tendency of a spiral spring which, if uncoiled and released, would snap back.

Ex. 149-155 show such melodic *elasticity,* the line rebounding after stepwise motion.

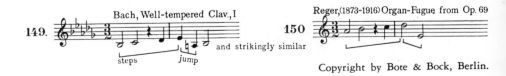

and strikingly similar

Pergolesi, (1710-1736) Stabat Mater

151. cu - jus   a - ni - mam ge - men - tem.

Okeghem, (1430-1495) Missa "Le Serviteur"

152. glo - ria   in   ex - cel - sis   De - o

A. Schönberg, "Gurre-Lieder"

153. triebst mich aus der   letz - ten   Frei - stadt

Copyright by Universal Edition, Vienna.
Reprinted by permission of Universal Edition & Associated Music Pub. Inc.

A. Schönberg, "Pierrot Lunaire"

154. kratzt   Pier - rot — auf sei - ner   Brat-sche

Copyright by Universal Edition, Vienna.
Reprinted by permission of Universal Edition & Associated Music Pub. Inc.

C. Saint-Saëns, "Samson and Dalila"

155. Et le re - tiens à mes — ge-noux!

Permission granted by Durand & Cie, Paris, and
Elkan-Vogel Co., Inc., Philadelphia, Pa., copyright owners

Ex. 156-171 show how a leap in the line is followed by stepwise motion in the opposite direction:

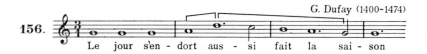

156. Le jour s'en - dort aus - si fait la sai - son

157. Las, je ——— ne puis

158. Nun sich der Tag ge - wen - det hat

159. Ju - bi - la ——— te

160.

161. Mozart, Quartet K. No. 428

(Note climax; see also page 67.)

162. Mozart, Quintet K. No. 516

163. Schumann, Piano-Quintet Op. 44

164. Mahler, 2nd Symphony

165. ibidem

Reprinted by permission of the copyright owners in the U. S. A.
Boosey & Hawkes, Inc., 668 Fifth Avenue, New York City

166. Mahler, 8th Symphony

Copyright by Universal Edition, Vienna.

167. Mahler, 8th Symphony

(See page 92ff.)

Permission granted by Durand & Cie, Paris. and
Elkan-Vogel Co., Inc., Philadelphia, Pa., copyright owners

Ex. 172 to 179 show melodic elasticity operating in a chain of alternating directions:

schmäh-lich du be-strafst?

173.

a-ber wenn er sich eilt und um die Ek-ke läuft, so kann er viel-leicht noch

Alban Berg,"Wozzeck"

auf ei-nem Paar Lip-pen

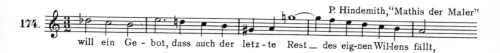

174.

will ein Ge - bot, dass auch der letz - te Rest — des eig-nen Wil-lens fällt,

P. Hindemith,"Mathis der Maler"

175.

C'est bon de re - spi - rer, c'est bon d'être a - vec toi, c'est

Milhaud,"Christophe Colomb"

bon de te sen - tir sur la face et sous les pieds!

Occasionally the slopes of a wave will show subdivisions, notches or indentations, as it were, the lines assuming an indented shape as shown in the following diagram:

180.

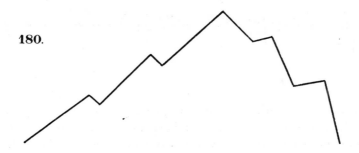

These notches will function as small halting or resting places within the main trend of the line, their locations largely determined by harmonic influences. They will show either mere halts (Ex. 198), or repetitions of harmonically marked tones (Ex. 181, 182),

181.

Bach, St. Matthew-Passion

Da nun Je - sus war zu Be - tha - ni - en

182.

Mozart,"Figaro"

In - gra - ta! nel mo-men-to del-la mia ce-re-mo-nia ei go-de-va leg-gen-do

or small figures using neighboring tones for embellishment (Ex. 183, 184),

183.

Bach, Well-temp. Clav., I

Mozart, Piano-Concerto K. No. 432

184.

(Note identity of structure!)

or even small recursions without prejudice to the principal direction. These latter will occur especially when the amplitude of the wave extends over a wider range, say beyond the interval of a tenth or so (Ex. 185-188). In such cases the notions "skip" and "step" assume a more relative meaning; within ranges as wide as those of Ex. 186 or 203, thirds and even an occasional fourth in the recoiling branch will still be felt as steps rather than as skips.

Chopin, Mazurka Op. 7 No. 1

185.

Chopin, Nocturne Op. 15 No. 2

186.

Beethoven, Violin-Sonata Op. 24

187.

(Compare also Ex. 167.)

Again the analogy with matters of form offers itself, as discussed on page 160.

The "wind-up"

If the wave starts with a skip, this skip is often preceded by a preparatory figure comparable to the motion we may make when getting ready for a throw—"winding up"—or for a jump—"taking a run". Such a preparatory figure will reveal a nervous, fidgeting character, a sort of wriggling before breaking loose; this character being produced by a group of short, quick notes, anything from a turn (mordent) to an independent, characteristic motif. The "winding up" motion is then followed by the "throw" or "jump", which in turn is followed by stepwise retrocession.

A few examples (189-197) may illustrate this feature.

(See also Ex. 134, bars 5 and 7; and Ex. 169, bar 2,
where the feature is reduced to a mere suggestion, while
wider leaps, such as in Ex. 193, 194 or 203, seem to call for
a stronger preparatory effort.)

In Ex. 195-197 this figure, still clear in its preparatory function, takes on a more personal character:

The preceding illustrations show how both components of melody, pitch-line and rhythm, collaborate to produce the nervous, wriggling character of the winding-up figure, in that small tone-intervals (stepwise motion) combine with small time-intervals (quick rhythms).

In Ex. 168 and 169 such a figure appears reduced to a rudiment of two sixteenths, still strong enough to convey the impression. (Similarly: Ex. 255).

Harmonic influence in the way of "notches" makes itself felt in Ex. 197. Here the winding-up motion becomes part of the skip itself, as though a temperamental bowler would run along for a stretch, before releasing the ball.

However, this collaboration of the two components, pitch-line and rhythm, is not confined to such preparatory figures, but penetrates the elements of "elasticity", skips and steps, as well.

Here is how the feature of elasticity shows in either component of melody:

What constitutes "stepwise progression" in the linear component, namely a series of small *line divisions,* corresponds in the rhythmical component to a series of small *time divisions*—fast progression, short notes. What constitutes the "skip" in the linear component, namely the fusion of a few small tone divisions into one big tone division, corresponds in the rhythmical component to the fusion of a few small time divisions into one big time division—slow progression, long notes.

Usually linear and rhythmical elasticity go together: Skips are performed in slow rhythms, small steps in fast rhythms (Ex. 198-203) .

198. Beethoven Str. Quartet Op. 18 No. 3

199. Mozart, Piano-Concerto K. No. 488

200. Mozart, "Magic Flute"

Dies Bild-nis ist be-zau-bernd schön, wie noch kein Au-ge je ge-seh'n!

The same correspondence is found in Ex. 141, 144, 153, 157, 159, 160, 162, 163, 164, 165, 166, 167, 168, 169, 170, 171, 172, 173, 174, 175, 176, 177, 181, 182, 185, 186, 188.

As to the skips, either both tones comprising them show slow progression (long notes), as in Ex. 153, 160, 163, 164, 166, 167, 171, 198, 202; or if the slow progression is confined to only one of them, it is usually the second, the one which *concludes* the skip; as though the line needed to catch its breath again after the exertion caused by the skip (Ex. 144, 156, 157, 162, 164, 167 (lower brackets) 168, 169, 170, 171, 172, 174, 176, 178, 185, 186, 190, 193, 196, 199, 200, 203, 208). Or else, the lapse of time may be produced or augmented by a rest, thereby still further increasing the impression that the line is panting for breath after the exertion of the skip (Ex. 166, 173 (!), 182, 183 (end), 184 (end), 195, 197, 204, 205, 209).

However, sometimes linear and rhythmical elasticity do not go together; i.e. elasticity may show only in one of the two components: either in the linear component alone (Ex. 149, 158, 161, 178, 179) or, in rarer cases, in the rhythmical component alone (Ex. 209).

If we give Ex. 204-209 a fleeting glance, we can **not** escape noticing the striking similarity of their structure.

A cursory first impression reveals as common features of their structure: (1) A starting segment of about four tones, marked by the seventh leap down. (2) A short rhythmical halt (or rest). (3) The "release", showing melodic elasticity of the last phrase.

To give the excerpts a common interpretation, just by feeling and impression:

A bunch of ants is dumped into a vessel (7th-leap down). Stunned for an instant (rest), they presently start scrambling up the walls.

Or:

Approach and occurrence of a collision (1). Numbed for a moment (2), everybody scrambles for safety (3).

Even the imaginary events of such interpretations suggest a sort of *psychical* elasticity, the accident not annihilating either ants or men, but causing increased activity and vitality.

Ex. 204-206 exhibit both linear and rhythmical elasticity in almost complete pureness. In Ex. 208 the elasticity in the rhythmical component of melody is somewhat stunted, while its counterpart, Ex. 209, shows elasticity confined only to the rhythmical component, the linear component yielding completely to the agency of harmony. In the double-fugue theme of Ex. 207 the feature splits into the rhythmical and linear component before our very eyes, the upper voice taking care of the linear half, unheedful of the rhythmical, the lower voice taking care of the rhythmical half, unheedful of the linear. The combination of the two voices produces the effect of both elements as though combined in a one-voiced melody, similar to Ex. 204, 205 and so many previous quotations.

CHAPTER VI

HOW HARMONY INFLUENCES MELODY

The more we proceed in our investigations on melody, the more we notice the influence of harmony on melody. Among the shaping forces in music, harmony and melody are the most closely related. To the superficial observer it may appear as though in the classical era harmony actually created melody, whereas in "modern" music melody actually creates harmony. But in reality this mutual impregnation is at work at all times, even though preponderance of one over the other may obtain at times. It is this mutual influence which incessantly promotes the evolution of each force, and with it, the broadening of each concept.

Ex. 210 shows clearly the melodization of harmony,

Mozart,"Eine Kleine Nachtmusik" K. No. 525

using the breaking of the two chief harmonies of the key for the creation of a melodic line. Such patterns of broken harmonies permeate innumerable classical themes, the quotation of which would fill books (see also Ex. 38, 92). Moreover, this method permeates classical composition itself, showing not only in the themes but also in accompanying and contrapuntal voices (Ex. 211, 212).

The use of "non-harmonic" tones breached the purity of the classical harmony system. All non-harmonic, or foreign tones (such as suspensions, appoggiaturas, anticipations, passing-, changing-, neighboring-tones, etc.) are invariably *melodic* events. So, at bottom, are alterations (melodically passing half-tones, foreign not only to the single harmony but also to the key). Though this book does not share the traditional approach to harmony, as demonstrated at length in the respective section, we may as well use these current terms for convenience.

With regard to harmony the rhythmic, or metric, location of non-harmonic tones is of no consequence. They change the color of the harmony in a definite direction irrespective of their metric position.

With regard to melody, however, it makes all the difference whether a non-harmonic tone occurs in a metrically. *accentuated* or in a metrically *unaccentuated* place.

Those nonharmonic tones which do *not* carry the metric accent have rather a playful, ornamental effect, leaving such melodies otherwise pretty close in character to the purely harmonic melodies (Ex. 213-216.)

Note the structural similarity of Ex. 213 to 215: The ascending tonic triad, its members all on accentuated beats, playfully surrounded by their neighbor-tones. Ex. 216 almost duplicates Ex. 215 in rhythm and in the placement of the harmonic and non-harmonic tones up to the half-cadence in bar 4, the only difference being the direction of the two lines.

However, if the non-harmonic tones carry the metric accent, that is if they appear on strong beats like suspensions and appoggiaturas, they give the melody a definite tint, esthetically and psychologically sharply contrasting with either purely harmonic melodies (such as Ex. 210) or with melodies using unaccentuated by-tones (such as Ex. 213-216).

The contrasting effect of accentuated and unaccentuated non-harmonic tones on the character of a melody is best illustrated if we juxtapose a representative of each type (Ex. 217, 218).

The constructive element of both melodies is a small, recurrent motif (indicated by ⌐——¬) which consists of one tone of the underlying harmony preceded by a few non-harmonic tones. Ex. 217 reveals all the harmonic tones as accentuated, in the light; while the by-tones are accentless, weightless, in the shade, amounting to mere grace notes in character and function. Ex. 218 reveals the harmonic tones as unaccentuated, in the shade, while the accents are invariably carried by non-harmonic tones, suspensions in character and function.

The masculine type and the feminine type

Melodies with unaccentuated, grace-note-like by-tones form substantially one group together with the melodies that consist of harmonic tones only, and we may put both varieties under the common heading of harmonic melodies; while melodies resting clearly on the use of accentuated, suspension-like non-harmonic tones, may briefly be called non-harmonic melodies.

Of the two sharply contrasting groups it can be said:

The psychological mark of the harmonic melody is directness, straightforwardness, simplicity, naturalness, manliness, masculine strength.

The psychological mark of the non-harmonic melody is veiledness, refinement, suspense, restraint, feminine tenderness, softness, the erotic touch ranging from tender yearning to flaring passion.

The "manly" type of melody shows in Ex. 219-221.

Beethoven, 3rd Symphony ("Eroica")

Mozart, Requiem ("Tuba Mirum")

It shows particularly in motifs of knights and heroes
(Ex. 261-264), in songs of masculine spirit such as marching,
drinking, hunting, fighting, patriotic songs (Ex. 222-235).

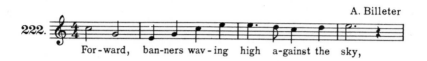

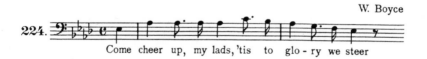

K. Wilhelm

227. Es braust ein Ruf wie Don - ner - hall,

Ludwig Fischer

228. Im küh-len Kel-ler sitz' ich hier auf ei - nem Fass voll Re-ben

Mozart, Don Giovanni

229. Finch' han dal vi - no cal - da la te - sta

u - na gran fe - sta fa pre - pa - rar.

Mozart, "Figaro"

230. Non più andrai far - fal - lo-ne a - mo - ro - so   not - te e

gior-no d'in-tor - no gi - ran - do, del - le bel - le tur-bando il ri -

po - so,   Nar - ci - set - to Adon-ci - no d'a - mor

Weber, "Freischütz" (Hunters' Chorus)

231.

John Stafford Smith

232.

Oh   say, can you see by the dawn's ear-ly   light,

Danish National Hymn

233.

Cuban National Hymn

234.

Swedish National Hymn

235.

The harmonic melody also expresses single-heartedness, artlessness, peace of mind (Ex. 236), nature, nearness to nature (Ex. 237-243) or to God (Ex. 244, 245), awe (Ex. 245), calm after the storm (Ex. 246, 247).

Largo   Haydn, Quartet Op. 76 No. 2

236

237.
Am Brun - nen vor dem To - re

238.
In ei-nem Bäch-lein hel-le, da schoss in fro-her Eil'

239.
Ich hört' ein Bäch-lein rau-schen wohl aus dem Fel-sen-quell,

240.
Das Wan-dern ist des Mül-lers Lust, das Wan-dern

241.
Komm, lie-ber Mai und ma - che die Bäu-me

242.

243.

244.

Si - lent night, ho - ly night, all is calm, all is bright.

Franz Gruber

245.

(Slow) Wagner, "Lohengrin"

(Chorus) Wie fasst uns se - lig süs - ses Grau - en!
What mys - tic awe is o'er us stream - ing!

246.

Beethoven, 6th Symphony

247.

Wagner, "Meistersinger" (Watchman's song, End of Act 2)

Hört, ihr Leut', und lasst euch sa-gen, die Glock' hat eil - fe ge-schla-gen:
Hark to what I say, good peo-ple; e - le - ven strikes from each steeple:

The "feminine" type of melody (Ex. 248-260), making ample use of accentuated non-harmonic tones, is revealed in themes of quiet, lyrical expression, in slow movements (Ex. 251, 252) or in passages of ebullient passion (Ex. 255).

248.

Mozart, Quartet K. No. 428

249. Mozart, Symphony K. No. 550

250. Mozart, "Magic Flute"
Ich fühl' es, ich fühl' es,

251. Adagio   Beethoven, Quartet Op. 59 No. 1

252. Andante   Beethoven, 9th Symphony

253. Brahms, Violin-Sonata Op. 100

254. (similar)   Brahms, Op. 105 No. 1
Wie Me-lo-di-en zieht es mir lei-se durch den Sinn

255. Weber, "Oberon"
Mein Hü-on, mein Gat-te, die— Ret-tung, sie naht!

Again it is the great psychologist Wagner who finds the most condensed expression, intensifying it still more by the interweaving of equally non-harmonic contrapuntal voices:

(See Ex. 22, 23, also 370.)

And again we see the manly type, the harmonic melody, juxtaposed in sharp contrast:

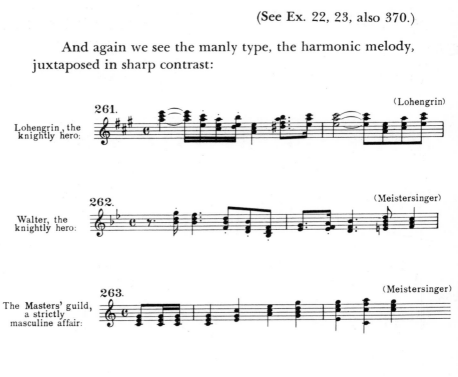

The knightly castle:

264.　　　　　　　　　　　　　　　　　　　(Tristan)

To be sure, the rhythmical component gives support to the psychic delineation: soft, flowing rhythms for the feminine type (256-260), clear cut, march-like rhythms for the masculine type, with a dash of squareness (263) or gallantry (261, 262, 264), respectively.

CHAPTER VII

DEFLECTIONS AND OTHER SPECIAL FEATURES

Related to the non-harmonic tones, and partly covering their appearance, is another feature of the melodic line which may be summed up under the heading of *deflection,* or *deviation.*

The deflection takes place either from the straight line (scale) or from the straight harmony (broken chord), in both cases irrespective of any metric position.

In Beethoven's Symphony No. 3 a glib version like Ex. 265 would easily suggest itself, the plain scale in bar 4 just filling the metric frame of the bar.

265.

Instead, Beethoven writes:

Beethoven, 3rd Symhony

266.

Compared with the neutral, colorless passage of Ex. 265 the animation and individualization of the line caused by the deflection is obvious.

Similarly he writes in his Fifth Symphony:

Beethoven, 5th Symphony

267.

It is interesting to know that his sketch-book, as edited by Nottebohm, shows the first shape of this theme as follows:

268.

Beethoven's correction makes it clear that he preferred the deflection even to the amenity of the suspension.

Deviation from straight harmony is evidenced in the countless "appoggiaturas" of classical melodies, such as Ex. 185, last bar, or Ex. 260.

The whole notes in Ex. 269 and 270 expose the harmonic skeletons of these lines:

269.

270.

Even where traditional harmonization, or tonality altogether, is denied, the line may still preserve its appoggiatura
character (Ex. 271).

Eugene Goossens, Quartet No. 2

271.

The encircling approach

The melodic effect of the deflection is enhanced when
both the low and high neighboring pitches, independent of
their order, are used for appoggiaturas and thus form an
encircling approach to the harmonic main tone before hit-
ting it. (See Ex. 217, 218, 252, before and after each bar line,
256, beginning of bar 4, 257, beginning of bar 6, 259, over
first bar line, 332, over second, fourth and sixth bar line, and
others). The theme of Ex. 371 represents, in its second bar,
a variant of particular piquancy, in that the encirclement is
put, not before but after the main tone, g♯. Thus the encircling approach is turned, as it were, into a diverging with-
drawal, bringing out still more plastically the deflection from
the harmonic-melodic basis of the c♯ minor triad.

The effect of the encirclement can be further enhanced
by extending the range of the appoggiatura beyond the immediate neighbor pitches, also by interpolating more than
just one tone before reaching the harmonic pitch. The
following quotation may serve as an illustration.

In bar 24 of Ex. 143 the last tone, *e,* has a strong tendency to proceed (resolve) to *f.* Yet the line deviates and forms an extended encirclement, a *loop,* as it were, around the harmonic tone, *f,* before reaching it, as indicated by the dotted lines (Ex. 272) :

The intensifying, particularizing effect of the feature becomes apparent.

Deflections may occur in chains, in a manner similar to sequences. The line will then take on the appearance of a two voiced passage, the individual melodic fragments alternatingly continuing in two different registers (Ex. 273-276), either in parallel motion (Ex. 273 ⌐B⌐, 274) or in opposite directions (Ex. 275, 276, 273 ⌐A⌐).

Bach, Organ-Fugue

Ernst Křenek, 2nd Symphony

Even the deviation from the straight scale appears sometimes in a chain, in that its subsequent steps are set up in
two different octaves (Ex. 277, 278):

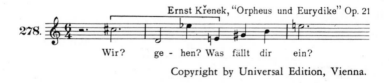

A. Schönberg, Violin-Concerto Op. 36

Ernst Křenek, "Orpheus und Eurydike" Op. 21

Wir?   ge - hen? Was fällt dir   ein?

It obviously lies in the nature of this feature to counter-
act the force of elasticity.

Iterances and elisions

On principle, a flowing melodic line will avoid the repetition of a pitch in too close a neighborhood, while its regis-
tering effect on our mind is still alive; just as, in linguistic
composition, the close recurrence of an expression affects us
somehow unpleasantly and we prefer to substitute a syno-
nym. The unpleasant effect, however, disappears as soon as

we feel the repetition to be planted with deliberation and purpose. (Cf. the same idea in connexion with the climax, page 85.) So used, the fault becomes a virtue. In fact, the iteration either of one tone or of a small group of tones (figure, motif) in identical metric and rhythmic configuration forms a melodic trait of considerable consequence.

Such *iterances,* as we may call them, are of partly tonal, partly rhythmic nature. They may occur either in immediate succession (Ex. 279-290) or separated by short interruptions (Ex. 291, 293).

They create or increase the most diverse moods, produce and intensify the most multicolored imagery.

The effect of impish sprightliness in Ex. 279-283 is largely due to iterances.

Iterances again give the special character to Ex. 284 and 285.

The popular "Fate" motif of Beethoven's Fifth Symphony (Ex. 108) would lose its significance if the three eighth notes were pitched in any other way than by merely repeating the same tone. This motif also shows how iterance elevates even the employment of no more than two different pitches to compelling pregnancy.

The same becomes clear from Ex. 286:

Iterance of one tone also shapes the motifs of Ex. 287 and 288,

Copyright 1896 by G. Ricordi & Co., Milano.

while the characteristics of Ex. 289-291 rest on iterance **of a**
figure:

Béla Bartók, Str. Quart. Op. 17

289.

Copyright by Universal Edition, Vienna.

Bach, Organ-Fugue

290.

Bach, Well-temp. Clav. I, Fugue 2

291.

If we try to replace the iterances of Ex. 291 by sequences, **as**
in Ex. 292,

292.

the face of the theme is gone, its individuality reduced to
staleness.

The first three bars of Ex. 293, compared with the first three bars of Ex. 195 reveal a remarkable similarity of structure.

Joseph Achron, First Violin-Sonata, Op. 29

293.

Here, as there: the beginning with the winding-up figure, made up of tone and by-tone iterance (bar 1), the leap upwards with ensuing rhythmical halt (bar 2), to be followed by a passage of tonal and rhythmic elasticity in bar 3. From here on the structures of the two quotations diverge. If we pursue Ex. 293 to its end, we see the iterances of bar 1 eclipsed by another iterance of far more telling effect: that of the loftily planted *e,* clinging doggedly to the pitch against all harmonic insinuations and hereby giving the theme **its** real clownish humor.

Iterances of the intermittent type sometimes take on the effect of what we may call a melodic fulcrum. The melody issues from a focal pitch (frequently but not necessarily the dominant) and returns to it repeatedly, moving either in one direction (Ex. 294-297)

or in opposite directions, which makes the fulcrum more a pivot or an axis (Ex. 298-302) :

Joh. Strauss, "Morning Journals" Op. 279

300.

Joh. Strauss, "The Beautiful Blue Danube" Op. 317

301.

César Franck, Piano-Quintet

302.

As a counterfoil to iterances, melody sometimes shows the complete absence, the *emphasized* absence of any tone, so to speak "accentuated rests". Such *elisions* constitute wilful interruptions of phrases, and thus give a motif or a melody-section a striking rhythmical touch. Their logical place is in the beginning or in the middle of the phrase, always on downbeats, or at least on accentuated beats.

Ex. 303b and 304b show by comparison the effect of the elision, in contrast to the continuous line as appearing in 303a and 304a.

Beethoven, 6th Symphony

303 a

Beethoven, Violin-Sonata Op. 23

303 b

Nicolai, "Merry Wives of Windsor"

304 a

(*transposed*)

Mozart, Quartet K. No. 428

304 b

(Cf. also Ex. 149, 150, 166, 184, 195)

Especially marked is the "thematic rest" on the down-beat (Ex. 305, 306).

Heitor Villa-Lobos, "Momo Precoce"

305.

Manuel De Falla, "La Vida Breve"

306.

In polyphonic composition where the plasticity of the theme is of particular significance, elisions play an essential part (Ex. 307-309).

Bach, Well-temp. Clav. I Fugue 16·

307.

(ibidem, Fugue 9)

308.

(ibidem, II No. 1)

309.

(Cf. also Ex. 183, 204, 209)

(Out of the 48 fugues of Bach's "Well-tempered Clavichord", 30 start with a rest on the downbeat of the first bar.)

Fugue themes are altogether the proper field for combined iterances and elisions (Ex. 310, 311).

Bach, Organ-Fugue

310.

William Schuman, "American Festival Overture"

311.

Copyright 1941 G. Schirmer, Inc.

(Cf. also Ex. 290, 291)

Though most effective in polyphonic style on account of the constant reappearance of the theme, the combination of iterances and elisions as a means of plastification holds its place in symphonic writing as well:

Haydn, Symphony

312

A. Dvořák, Symphony No. 5

313.

Copyright by N. Simrock.
Reprinted by permission of N. Simrock & Associated Music Pub. Inc.

An outstanding passage of combined iterances and elisions is presented in Ex. 314:

314.

Beethoven, Third Symphony

Note the frequency of the rests on the downbeats of bars 6-10 — *an iterance of elisions.* What chords could match these rests in eloquence and impressiveness? The deep rifts precisely on these downbeats are a thematic resource of highest expressive power. The very absence of any sound constitutes an audible effect of contrast, comparable to the visual effect of the blank spots the etcher or silhouettist would use for constrast. Bars 10-13 represent a kind of a stretto in which rests as well as chords form iterances, opposing each other in a struggle for predominance. Halting all harmonic or melodic progressions, this exciting passage rests entirely on the effect of iterances and elisions.

COUNTERPOINT

"... that action and counteraction which from the reciprocal
struggle of discordant powers draws out the harmony of the
universe"

Edmund Burke, *"Reflections on the Revolution of France"*

CHAPTER VIII

THE MEANING OF COUNTERPOINT

Perhaps it is the somewhat cryptic term itself which accounts for the fact that, among all the branches of the "gray theory" of music, counterpoint sounds the most theoretical, the most scientific, the most cryptic. The innocent layman would rather link the term to higher mathematics or physics than to a thing as live, serene and lovely as music. Just as melody must be a matter of sheer inspiration, probably counterpoint is a matter of sheer speculation — the one as close to nature as the other far from it.

Theory derives the term from "punctum contra punctum", or "point against point", adding that "punctum" once had the meaning of a musical note and therefore counterpoint means "note against note". This explanation is supposed to be very old, going back to the first attempts at singing in several parts. Just exactly which learned personage is responsible for this explanation, seems to be another mystery; nevertheless it is adhered to religiously and deferentially up to the present day and it certainly leaves us none the wiser.

In the first place, notwithstanding the historic origin of the term, the real nature of counterpoint is anything *but*

"note against note", even in strict sixteenth century counterpoint where such application would cover only the first of
the redoubtable "five species"—the one which *in practice*
hardly played any role at any time. Besides, does it not seem
rather far-fetched to bring the *second* "point" into the definition at all? Does—or did at any time—"afternoon" mean
"noon after noon"? Does "undertaker" mean *"taker* under
taker"? Why then must counterpoint mean *point* counter
point? Finally, if "punctum", or "point", had at one time the
connotation of a musical note, it surely had *at all times* the
meaning of *topic* or *subject.* And while the ancient interpretation seems to accentuate the "point" part, we definitely
prefer to shift the emphasis to the "counter" part of the term.
This makes counterpoint simply the *point of contrast;* and
the only reason why such a simple explanation is nowhere
to be found must be that it would make things too easy, and
would deprive the term of its scientific aura.

Suppose a stage play should start by showing a loving
couple happily embracing one another, and from the wings,
left and right, should enter the respective parents and give
their blessings, and then the curtain should fall again. We
certainly would revolt at such preposterousness. What we
would miss, and eagerly demand to see, is the various hap-
penings *in point of contrast.*

A meeting of any kind will hardly take its course with
every one nodding assent to the speaker's discourse and leaving thereafter. Rather, it will produce a discussion *in point
of contrasting ideas,* voicing the pros and cons, and thus resulting in clarification and final shaping of the issue. Herein
lies the virtue of the "healthy opposition": it becomes a
means not of obscuration but of clarification, not of obstruc-
tion but of propulsion.

Apply these considerations to music and you get the real, intrinsic meaning of counterpoint, one of the most powerful *shaping forces in music;* we might even go so far as to say, one of the most powerful shaping forces in art altogether.

When in Wagner's "Meistersinger" the crowd of Nuremberg citizens comments on Beckmesser, one group ridiculing his pitiful appearance while another group is still impressed by his high civic rank, the opposition of the two groups obtains musical support by the contrapuntal treatment of the passage (Ex. 315):

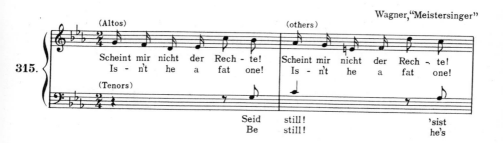

315.

Scheint mir nicht der Rech - te!   An der Toch-ter Stell' ich   den nicht möch-te!
Is - n't he a fat one!   In the la - dy's place I'd   not have that one!

Witz!   Der hat im Ra - te Stimm' und Sitz!
prate!   He is a learn - ed ma - gi - strate!

(English version by H.& F. Corder)

Thus the example illustrates in a *double* way, by word and tone, the nature of counterpoint: opposition, contradiction, fighting. The two opposed musical lines reveal the chief weapons of this fight, the two chief means of contrapuntal expression: Contrast in rhythm and contrast in the direction of movement. When one voice is in repose, the other moves on; when one voice moves up, the other moves down.

If the words were spoken in their exact rhythms instead of sung, at least one of these fundamentals of counterpoint, rhythmical contrast, would still be distinctly felt.

The above considerations make it clear that, rather than "note against note", counterpoint means the simultaneous presence of two (or more) contrastingly *moving* voices, or as we may say, *melodic lines*.

As such the musical phenomenon of counterpoint is familiar to us from countless experiences. Let us now, for further investigation, single out one of those familiar acquaintances:

Bach, Two Part Invention

316.

Bar 1 of Ex. 316 shows a moderately fast motion with upward moving tendency. Imitated in the lower voice in bar 2, the upper line now puts up a typical counterpoint against the lower one: distinct rhythmical contrast, distinct downward motion. The same procedure repeats in bar 3, with the order of the voices reversed. Bar 4 keeps only to one of the fundamentals of counterpoint, namely the rhythmical contrast. So does bar 7 again, while bars 5 and 6, in absolute parallelism both rhythmically and tonally, completely upset the sacred "rules" of counterpoint. The same happens almost throughout the whole of bar 9.

Is it, then, that Bach did not know even the fundamental rules of counterpoint? Or was he just negligent when writing these "false" bars, or did he do it for mere mischief and spite, "pour épater le bourgeois", as the French say?

We cannot deny that the piece is utterly charming, including, *to say the least,* these wrong bars.

Two children play at catch, or hide and seek, the pursued every once in a while teasing the pursuer in a demonstrative challenge.

Two butterflies are engaged in a flirtation, chasing each other, yet once in a while flying together for a stretch in a coquettish mock-truce, until one breaks loose again and provokes the other into resuming the chase.

By slackening the tension of "counterpoint" for a short while these arraigned bars render the ensuing resumption of the chase the more effective. The unexpected cessation of the intrigue becomes an intrigue in itself, like the feinting retreat of a fencer. The passage takes the effect of counterpoint *inside* of counterpoint; opposing the opposition, contradicting the contradiction.

So strong is the effect of this feature that it holds good even in the rigorous structure of a fugue, consolidating the parallelism to its limit, the unison:

Bach, Well-temp. Clav. I, Fugue X

317.

At the bottom of this feature lies the principle that any quality is apt to weaken and to lose its effect after a while; and the best preventive for that is an offsetting and reanimating intermission. This observation touches upon the basic "tension—relaxation" principle of form, as treated in the following section.

However, this is not the only point which links counterpoint with form, in fact makes counterpoint a powerful functional agent of form.

CHAPTER IX

ORNAMENTAL AND FERMENTATIVE COUNTERPOINT

Counterpoint does not always exhibit the same **appearance and** function. We may discriminate between two **main trends** of counterpoint which not only differentiate its **quality and** nature but also have a bearing on its evolution.

In external appearance the difference may perhaps be **best** described by the fact that the one type is **principally based** on close thematic or motivic unity of the **opposing voices,** while the other type does not keep to such unity but **either** slackens it considerably or drops it altogether. The **first** kind represents the *imitative* type, covering the epoch of **polyphonic** writing which climaxes in canon and fugue. Here **counterpoint** has a predominantly ornamental function; or-**namental** in a broad sense, as an architectural designation **and** with no prejudice to the personal depth of the composer or the profundity of contents of the composition. The other type of counterpoint spurns the ornamental quality and favors a function which we may rather describe as stirring, or *fermentative*. With respect to formative power we may say that the ornamental type of counterpoint is to a lesser degree a shaping force than the fermentative type is.

Ornamental counterpoint, the altogether prevailing form of expression during the hey-day of polyphonic writing, became the theater of a particular technical skill. It is, up to the present day, the only type of counterpoint with which traditional study deals. Though a source of utter delight in the hands of a real tone-*poet* like Bach or Mozart, it carries the danger of degenerating into an idle sport or, worst of all, into dry pedantry—"paper-music". If, before attempting to write a fugue, we would take the trouble to investigate, we would find that Bach almost never carries the first appearance of a theme throughout a whole fugue, and that he constantly keeps applying far-reaching changes to his themes and counter-themes. We would thus become more conscious of dealing not with a skilful technical routine but with tone-poetry which just happens to employ the preferred idiom of the period.

Fermentative counterpoint escapes the danger of pedantry to a great extent by being based on continuous free, inventive creation which shields the composer from the traps of technicalities.

The real orginator and great pro-fessor of fermentative counterpoint is Richard Wagner.

Small wonder that the expert professors declared his way of using—abusing, rather, in their eyes—the hallowed craft rank dilettantism. They were at least not wrong in sensing that this kind of counterpoint, though still undeniably felt as counterpoint in the sense of contrastingly moving voices, was a different art from what counterpoint used to be hitherto by its very nature. For this very nature was definitely of the ornamental type, worshipping at the shrine of imitation and therefore clinging to the texture of tight motivic unity. Even where Wagner approaches the ornamental type, as in the mock-fugue (bar 138ff.) or the three theme stretto (bar 158ff.) of the "Meistersinger" Prelude, it is as though he would frivolously flirt with the austere craft, would nod a lofty, insulting "hello" to the redoubtable academy. For the rest of this piece, however, almost throughout it from beginning to end, the contrapuntal treatment discards the principle of dense motivic unity, the imitative style, and replaces it with the principle of motivic independence, of freely progressing, continuously renewing "infinite melody". Counterpoint takes on a new, strong, individual function: it becomes the leaven, the ferment, the very *stuff of fermentation;* it acts as the agent of promotion, propulsion, *formation.* At the same time it changes the character of the music from spiritual lucidity to brewing emotionalism.

The limits of this book do not permit the reproduction of a piece of such dimensions as would be necessary to demonstrate all this in detail. It is strongly recommended that one listen attentively and repeatedly to a good recording of the entire Prelude, alternately with and without the use of a score.

So strongly is the difference of the two types of counterpoint felt, that passages like the two mentioned above (bar 138ff. and bar 158ff.), by their mere approach to ornamental counterpoint, have, in their environment, a similarly relaxing effect to that which the passages of parallelism in Ex. 316 and 317 have in their environment of ornamental counterpoint. Parallelism is to ornamental counterpoint what ornamental counterpoint is to fermentative counterpoint.

Bach and Wagner represent the chief exponents of music which is essentially rooted in polyphonic conception, or counterpoint; ornamental or fermentative, respectively. Their music does not *apply* counterpoint; it derives its very life and breath from it. Between them, temporally as well as ideologically, lies the type of music represented in the symphonic style of the eighteenth and nineteenth century, which attempts to combine homophonic and polyphonic writing and to reconcile both basic concepts.

The great exponent of this style is Mozart. With him too, as with Bach and Wagner, counterpoint is not an accessory, but an *intrinsic part* of the creative mechanism. Yet, going through the alembic of his mind, counterpoint again takes on an individual quality and function. Both Mozart and Wagner are true disciples of Bach; but by dint of their strong personalities the common tool, counterpoint, is bent and shaped in the directions their individual minds work. And it appears that while Wagner's counterpoint becomes functional towards *fermentation* and—in the wake of it— *emotionalism*, Mozart's counterpoint, directed the opposite way, becomes functional towards *crystallization*, serenity and *spiritualism*.

A few bars—Ex. 318 and 319—may reveal these respective qualities in a condensed form, as in a microscopic blood-test, so to speak. Ex. 318 shows bars 67 to 75 of Wagner's "Meistersinger" Prelude, Ex. 319 bars 58 to 67 of Mozart's Overture to "The Magic Flute".

Counterpoint, the agent of fermentation: Wagner

Counterpoint, the agent of crystallisation: Mozart

The excerpts also show how the respective orchestrations underline the two contrasting functions of counterpoint. The Mozartean use of counterpoint combines with the preservation of pure, unadulterated sound-colors towards crystallization and cool spirituality. The Wagnerean use of counterpoint combines with the creation of alloyed, blended sound-colors towards fermentation and intoxicating sensuality.

Thus counterpoint infiltrates even orchestration; its diverging tendencies duplicate in orchestration.

Apart from these observations, it becomes clear that counterpoint is just as much subject to constant evolution and flux as is melody and harmony, with which it is indissolubly interwoven.

If Bach, Mozart and Wagner are three individual masters of counterpoint, they are wellnigh masters of three individual arts.

Intrinsic and integrant as counterpoint is with these composers, it still does not constitute so elementary a musical factor as do for instance melody and harmony, without which hardly any kind of articulate music is conceivable. The participation in the use and development of contrapuntal writing is to a high degree an individual and personal matter among composers. It in no way belittles the value of Debussy's, Puccini's or Johann Strauss' works that their minds did not primarily work in the direction of contrapuntal thinking.

And yet, the idea of counterpoint is apt to tint even a musical inspiration of the most unsophisticated nature.

If Strauss writes:

the little superimposed figure is certainly neither relative to the melody nor to the accompaniment. What it indicates is a last rudimentary trace of counterpoint, still clearly showing its characteristics of rhythmical contrast and contrary motion.

FORM

"*The very essence of life is movement*"
Jack London, "*The Sea Wolf*"

CHAPTER X

THE BASES OF FORM

Whatever FORM may be, let us not confuse it with *forms,* namely, the forms used in classical music. These forms generally constitute what is taught and studied under the heading of "form", frequently augmented by "analysis", though the "analysis" also means nothing else than the analysis of these forms. This study will enable one to tell whether a piece of the classical period is written in the form of Sonata, Rondo, Variation, etc.

But if a composer for any reason would like to break away from them, and, at the same time, *the forms* are the only thing he knows about FORM, he must necessarily feel pretty much lost. And if a student who knows all the terms and what they stand for is confronted with a piece of music that happens to follow none of these standard models, all his knowledge of form plus analysis will be of no avail to him. Does this mean that such a piece has no form at all?

Besides, what is the form of a Prelude, a Fantasy, a Nocturne, a Berceuse, a Kyrie, a Love Duet? And for that matter, what is the form of most of our contemporary "Sonatas" or "Symphonies", in spite of their traditional titles?

A piece may be written in any one of the classified forms to its minutest detail and still may exhibit a pitifully poor FORM.

And a piece may reveal not the slightest affiliation to any of the traditional forms, and yet may be a prodigious master-piece of FORM.

FORM is to forms as the universe is to a mountain or a tree.

How would you describe the form of a fugue? Among the wealth of Bach's fugues no two show the same structure. Yet each of them displays a masterly FORM, be it macrocosmically majestic or microcosmically graceful and dainty.

In highest art content and form coincide. How, then, could FORM be reduced to a few forms when content is limited only by the universe?

True, in the heyday of classical music, most of it was written in the traditional forms, mainly the sonata form. This was comparatively new and young; it was a good frame, firm enough and yet flexible enough; and it had evolved *for good reasons,* as had the smaller and lighter forms, too. The great masters did not need to bother further about these forms, for they had plenty to say, plenty to fill the frames anew and anew with their original, personal ideas; so much so that they unwittingly kept contributing to their further development, modifying them, deflecting them, bending them under the will of their individual genius. For the small talent, however, they were just welcome vehicles, easy tracks to follow, apt to turn FORM into formalism and pedantry. And what else but formalism and pedantry is it if theory keeps teaching analysis of the few forms? Is it a worthy goal to the creative mind to know that this piece is written in sonata form, that in rondo form? *Who cares?* Surely not the composer. Surely not the performer. Surely not the audience.

Research should not stop at describing some surface appearances and putting tags and labels on them. Nor will such knowledge ever help a creative talent to express himself musically.

It was said above that composition of the past arrived at some forms, or frames, *for good reasons.* Let us try to investigate these reasons instead of the forms; the sources and forces at work below the surface, instead of the surface. And let us see if these forces do not apply to composition at large, beyond the frames developed so far.

The meaning of form

Schopenhauer calls architecture "frozen music". This is not merely an aesthetic comparison; the analogy goes into the very substance of both arts. By the same token one could call music "sounding architecture". The "measure" is essential for both to such an extent that music borrows the very term for its metrical units. Architecture in turn uses the "motif", another kind of unit, as a germ-cell for building purposes—just as music does—by reiteration, modification, combination, grouping and regrouping. Perfect **FORM** crowns the masterpiece of architecture as well as the masterpiece of music.

Yet, while architecture unfolds itself in the medium of *space,* the medium in which music unfolds itself is *time.*

Concentrating on the subject of music, let us consider the qualities and characteristics of time.

Time rolls on uniformly, uninterruptedly, unceasingly. Units add to units, to form bigger units, unceasingly. Seconds accumulate to minutes, to hours, to days, weeks, months, years, decades, centuries. At the bottom of time operates a monotonous rhythm, mirrored in our own being by the beat of our heart, the pulsation of our bloodstream.

This regularly reiterant rhythm forms, as it were, a bottommost stratum of which we become conscious only at rare intervals.

Above this nethermost stratum lies and works another stratum: the periodical alternation of contrast.

While seconds, minutes, hours roll on in constant equality, at the same time there is a constant alternation of day and night, winter and summer, low tide and high tide. While the fundamental rhythm of pulsation accompanies us continuously, at the same time we alternate in exhalation and inhalation, in the consciousness of being awake and the unconsciousness of sleep.

It is the interplay of these two elementary forces that builds and feeds the skeleton of music. Primitive music may be satisfied with the basic element, the rhythm. The reiteration of a definite rhythmical pattern, produced mainly, if not solely, by percussion instruments, will create a certain stirring effect. Inspired by bodily movements, and inspiring bodily movements, like marching or dancing, it may be protracted at random, may give suitable support to such performances, may create certain moods and even a kind of primitive mental ecstasy. But it will never create *musical form,* no matter how complicated, intricate and refined such rhythmical patterns may be. For that, the second element has to be added: the element of *contrast,* of black and white, of light and shade, of *tension and relaxation.* It is the right distribution of light and shade, or of tension and relaxation, that is formative in every art, in music as well as in painting, sculpture, architecture, poetry.

In the development of musical form the force of contrast, the alternation of tension and relaxation, more and more restrained the primordial force of the rhythmical pulsation to the background, to the undermost stratum, keeping it there, as it were, tamed and subdued. And though the interplay of the two forces will always have its bearing on form, we may, in the interest of terseness, confine ourselves to the definition of FORM as the *balance between tension and relaxation.*

The more equilibrated this balance is, the better will be the form of a musical piece. Thus it becomes clear that form will always be largely a matter of feeling, not to be pinned down like the signature of a key or the *established forms.* Yet, this feeling for form can be aroused, developed and fortified in the student of composition. It must be stated here, however, that when we speak of balance we by no means mean a half and half distribution of the contrasting elements. On the contrary, as we will soon see, the proportion, if expressed in measuring terms, will always favor the tension segment as against the relaxation segment.

In Ex. 321 a rhythmical pattern of four bars is sounded four times in succession:

"The Lorelei"(Fr. Silcher, 1838)

Apart from the last repetition in which bar 2 shows a slight change (♩ ♪ instead of ♩.), the pattern keeps repeating without any change (Ex. 322):

The third phrase, by ascending to the key of the domi-nant and resting (cadencing) on it temporarily, creates a certain tension, as though a weight should be lifted and should accumulate potential energy, eager to be released again. This release back to the previous level (the tonic of the key) takes place in the following (fourth) phrase—the relaxation after the tension. Or, the effect of phrases 3 and 4 may be compared to the bracing effect of our inhalation and the relaxing effect of our exhalation, respectively.

Should we stop the melody at the end of the third phrase, we would intensely feel the "call" of the tonic, *g*— its power of attraction. The harmonic-melodic figure of the accompanying middle voices here (bar 4 of the third phrase) gives distinct support to this "home-calling" tendency. It works as a bridge, preparing and heralding the following section with all its implications. These joints have a particularly delicate task and function in FORM, as we will soon see.

From the viewpoint of the theory of *forms,* Ex. 321, on account of its structure and its measurements, is a specimen of what is termed the "two-part song-form", and that is that.

From the viewpoint of FORM the little song reveals, in the nucleus, the interplay of the undercurrent forces that make for FORM, *any form,* regardless of measurements and their resulting terms, regardless of epoch and style; just FORM as an artistic vessel, or garment of musical expression —in short, composition.

It was mentioned before that the definition of FORM as the balance between tension and relaxation does not imply an equal ratio of the sections devoted to each of the two elements, but that in mere temporal extent the former preponderates over the latter. That, too, shows in the little form of Ex. 321, where only the last quarter of the song, phrase 4, covers the relaxation part. It would be wrong to believe that the tension part, taking place in phrase 3, is equal in length to the relaxation part. For as stated above, the creating motive for both is the rising to the dominant (D major) and the falling back to the tonic (G major). But without the preceding phrases 1 and 2, the key of G major would not be established; without the key being established, phrase 3 could not be felt as a *rise* to its dominant, nor phrase 4 as a return to it, and therefore the tension-relaxation effect must collapse. (By the same token the sounding of the high *g,* in both phrases 1 and 2, is the premise of the climax of the melodic line, the high *b,* in its last quarter and close to its end). Thus the portion of the ascent, both in form and melodic line, outweighs the portion of the descent considerably.

Larger forms

A side-glance at the construction of a drama will help to illustrate and interpret this phenomenon. The drama, too, unfolds itself through the medium of time, and uses the mechanism of logical and psychological consecution. Here a plot is created, developed, lifted from level to level by continuously added intrigues, the ascending line covering the predominant portion of its range; until in the last (often short) act, the intricate threads disentangle, and no superflous wordiness hampers the precipitation to the end.

The comparison with the drama, though applicable as an overall principle to small forms like Ex. 321, intensifies with the larger musical forms. As the drama will not roll on uninterruptedly, but subdivide into smaller sections—acts, scenes—so the larger musical form, even if still in one movement, will provide, by subdivisions, for resting points and breathing spaces. And while the short descending line will be relatively straight and taut, the long ascending line, ascending as a whole, will show curves, notches, retarding moments, similar to those of the melodic line (Ex. 134). A tragedy will not loosen its grip after the climax; but before it, on the long way up to it, provision might well be made for some temporary, refreshing laughs. They will help the reader or spectator to brace himself for the ever tightening grip of the plot; and interspersed as welcome little spots of contrast, they will prevent the interest in the main problem from flagging and tiring. In the same way a light comedy, straight to the point after the climax, will benefit by weaving into the ascending section an occasional musing contemplation or a similar incidental excursion into the more serious and weighty.

In musical form these little contrasts within the main trend are not felt as impairing the drive; on the contrary, they set it off to better advantage, giving each section a new impetus.

A masterpiece of form will reveal these qualities even though it may follow none of the classical forms and may therefore deny any traditional approach of formal analysis.

Listen to a good recording of Wagner's "Meistersinger" Prelude; first let it just affect you, then listen again with a score or piano-score.

The almost constantly ascending line covers the overwhelmingly major part of the piece, up to bar 211. The following diagram (Ex. 323) may illustrate its periods of tension and relaxation. The numbers refer to the respective bars, and the idea is to mark these bars in the piano score before reading it together with a recorded or live performance.

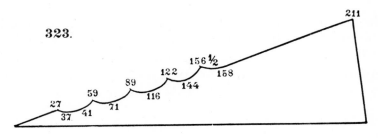

323.

The ascending fragments of the line tend to preserve the key (C major) and the pushing, driving, vigorous, masculine character. The receding fragments provide the change of mood (lyrical, feminine in bars 27-37, 89ff; grave, impressive in 59ff; humorous, mocking in 122ff) which is also largely supported by change of key.

With the exception of the sudden change at 122, the indentations do not appear as pronounced as in the diagram; rather they are softened by smooth modulations and occasional bridges (37-41, 89-97). A constant undercurrent of moving contrapuntal voices, often supported by or resulting in massed, tension-charged harmonies, keeps driving, urging, rolling the masses like molten metal in the process of founding, and constantly building, building, building. Each of the mounting fragments marks the achievement of a higher level, until, in a broad, last, irresistible sweep (158-211) a gigantic, crushing climax is reached, triumphant like the hoisting of the victorious flag in conquered territory. From this peak, the piece plunges to its end in a few bars.

Wagner was often accused of making a hodgepodge, a potpourri of the themes contained in his operas, for their respective overtures. In "Rienzi" he still kept to the traditional overture in the sonata form. But feeling somehow restrained in his personal ideas by this—or probably any—traditional form, he created his own form and mastered it. True, he used the themes of the opera for material. But why should such material be less fit for perfect form, if tamed and subjugated by the master's hand? And if it is true that in highest art, content and form coincide (which means that inspiration creates its own form) it is equally true that form as a tool—self-created or accepted—retroactively can have an inspiring effect on the artist, as even the mere objective tool may have—the blank manuscript paper, canvas or marble block.

So in a piece like the "Meistersinger" Prelude, form is neither a loose potpourri nor just the "grouping of a given thematic material", as the notion of form is frequently defined. Irregular and unruly in every detail as it seems to be, akin nowhere in detail or *in toto* to any of the traditional forms, its form is compellingly, irresistibly, inescapably present—omnipresent, *sovereign,* responding in the highest degree to *the shaping forces in music.*

A promise is given in the beginning of the piece which is magnificently fulfilled in the end. A goal is set up which, approached step by step in constant onward drive, is gloriously reached. We set out in venturesome youth and, seasoned by the events of the journey, we return wise and mature.

In such interpretations by way of feeling and touch, we may approach such nondescript, yet ever so present form. At the same time, while none of the traditional forms is catalogued by this approach, a most important basic principle is revealed: The principle of *tripartition.* To it most of the forms can be traced, regardless of their substructures, proportions, standards, terms.

It is of little concern whether we call the three parts exposition, development and reprise, or the sections of the three-part song-form, or Menuetto, Trio and da Capo, or just A B A^1. The affinity and correlation of the flanking parts will always be felt as against the middle part, the bearer of intensification, plot, *contrast.* Whence we came, thither we return, after all the blooming and climaxing, after all the turbulence and trepidation. The principle of tripartition, as manifest in art, is rooted in nature, in our souls, in our very existence.

And here is where the "formless" Meistersinger Prelude touches classical form—in the high-levelled, if epitomized, reprise and coda (measure 188 to the end) of its missing "Sonata".*

It is easy enough to see that the principle of tripartition also applies to a piece as small as Ex. 321. Phrases 1 and 2 obviously make up one coherent part, as against phrase 3, the contrasting middle part, and phrase 4, the reprise. Flatly, there is no such a thing as a two-part song-form. What makes song-form as such the prototype of the tripartite form, is simply the presence of a contrasting middle section between two analogous flanking sections, irrespective of any number of bars or any other tabulations. To divide song-form into one two-part, and one three-part song-form is like dividing the family of dogs into a group of dogs with four legs, and a group of dogs with a wart on the left jowl.

Small as the curve of the little phrase 3 (Ex. 321) is, it deserves all the interest and all the credit for bringing about FORM. Here, in this middle section of the song-form, is the place for the tension so essential for good form.

The following example may illustrate how high this curve, scarcely more than an indication in Ex. 321, may bulge and vault in the master's hand to result in utterly delightful, masterly form.

---

* It may be mentioned here that the term "Sonata" originally meant nothing else than played music, instrumental music, *musica sonata* as contrasted to sung music, vocal music, *musica cantata*.

Allegretto

Schubert, Menuetto from Octetto Op. 166

324.

The composer could easily have satisfied the academic requirements by entering the reprise after the half-cadence in bar 18. The modulation back to the tonic was consummated, nothing was in the way of the return.

Instead, what happens? Ignoring the easy path, the passage swerves to a remote key and from there, traveling through ever new keys (25-33) soars high up, to land again on the dominant (bar 33) and to enjoy now, *only now,* the infinitely more gratifying reprise.

And while we are on the subject: Again it would have been easy to make the conventional reprise, perhaps concluding it in the main key by merely transposing the last four bars (9, 10, 11, 12) into F major. Nothing of the kind happens. First of all the theme itself is diverted right after the first pair of bars. And now, like a faint reverberation of the preceding surge, the tide again rises in threefold sequence (38ff) until it breaks upon the unexpected D major triad (43). Nonplussed, as it were, the passage turns back and, groping about in utmost tenderness, floats down, and, finally, *only now,* home.

What is this? An "episode"? An "extension"? Any other standard device?

Anything can be an extension, if, in such a classification, we are satisfied to include any insertion of a larger or smaller number of additional bars. Under such circumstances, the formative function of such additional bars can be utterly meaningless, and their classification under any heading can be as futile as an identical equation or an identical definition.

What elevates these two "extensions" of the Schubert Menuetto to the real function of creating, not *a* form, but FORM, is the fact that they, precisely they, are the very theater of the tension-relaxation duel, which we cannot escape feeling when we listen to the piece.

Here we see inspiration molded into sublimest form and, equally, form elevated to sublimest inspiration—the consummate absorption of each by the other.

Form versus number

It seems pertinent to remind ourselves again that proportions in artistic form, especially in musical form, do not coincide with arithmetical ones. We observe, on the contrary, that mathematical symmetry is rather apt to render form stiff and dead, and that, indeed, it is the barely perceptible irregularities which infuse life into artistic form. To be sure, it takes the subtlety and refinement of the accomplished artist to sense the appropriate places and quotas of the irregular.

In listening to the above Schubert Menuetto, one certainly gets the impression of the minutest equilibrium of form, both *in toto* and in detail. Yet the piece embraces a number of measures as odd as 55. Starting from the standard classical period of four or eight bars, one would arrive at this figure by such even greater oddities as 13 times 4 plus 3, or 7 times 8 minus 1. A closer investigation reveals that the deviations from the "regular" occur in precisely the two passages that cause so much delight: the first, through the timid, echo-like repetition of bar 26; the second, through the unexpected contraction of an expected four bar span into the startled hastiness, as it were, of the solitary bar 43.

A cursory glance at the bar numbers of Ex. 323 shows a far greater inequality of the sections, though it is no more conspicuous when the piece is actually played. The composition offers but one traditionally built eight-bar period, namely, the beginning of the march theme, bars 41-49. It is answered here by a 10 bar clause, while the answer of its restatement (188) loses itself in a high-arched climax, piling up disparate masses during a total of 15 bars. The first section of the piece (up to 27) consists, by a strange and amazing coincidence, of two *equal* subdivisions, each 13 bars long— their parity manifestly wholly accidental. And so it goes on, elevating irregularity to blessed law.

Though this persistency of the irregular is part of a highly personal style in the case of Wagner, classical literature is rife with similar, if more scattered, incommensurabilities.

The following example (325) may demonstrate how inspiration defies mathematical reasoning in the structure, not of a piece, but of a single theme.

325.

Mendelssohn, Violin-Concerto

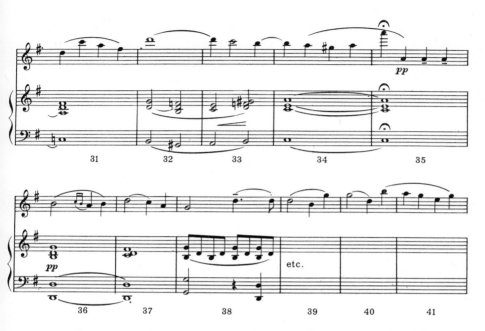

Any attempt to restore mathematical symmetry in this theme must lead to the destruction of its wonderfully arched contour. There is no doubt that the three equal quarter-notes of bar 1 have the full weight of the arsis, as against the lesser weight of bar 2—thesis—of the metric construction. Yet gradually and imperceptibly this relation shifts. The three quarter-note figure, still in full arsis-character in bars 9, 11, 13, assumes more and more the up-beat tendency of the thesis, first in bar 17, more in 25, altogether in 35. The last instance, accentuating the downbeat of 36, makes bar 38 appear as though it were a contraction of two bars, with the entrance of the following theme coming in one bar too soon. Similarly, bar 25 blends thesis (after 24) and arsis (before 26) into one, thus anticipating the entrance of the theme by one bar. The part of the solo violin, drifting at this juncture in a lovely counterpoint to the theme, takes the lead soon again, mounting to a climax, unheedful of any considerations of structural symmetry.

CHAPTER XI

THE ART OF JOINING

The observation of such contractions as in the previous example, blending the end of an expiring phrase into the beginning of a new one, brings us closer to the subject of the "joints".

The ways of combining major or minor sections of a whole, the various transitions, retransitions, re-introductions, and the like, play an essential role in the matter of form. The joints are truly the spots where artistry meets artisanship, where genius meets technique, where the com-poser becomes the joiner.

As in oratory, drama and architecture, they are the spots of smooth transition, of unbroken flow, of linking preservation of movement. As in oratorical, dramatic or architectural structure, they are the spots to reveal taste, refinement and inventiveness in the hand of the skilful, or inept clumsiness in the hand of the unskilled.

Though the principle of overlapping and interlocking is common and basic to these joints, it works in manifold ways and takes on various appearances.

The method of telescoping a concluding section with a beginning, as suggested in bar 25 of Ex. 325, becomes clearly apparent in the following quotation (Ex. 326).

326.

Mozart, Symphony K. No. 550

We would rather expect the transition to be as follows:

But the theme comes in sooner, carried pickaback, as it were, by the cadential bassoon passage of bars 20 and 21, and arriving in impatient anticipation at its second bar by the time the cadence is completed. The same device reoccurs at the beginning and at the end of the development of this movement. There, the transition, gliding down delicately on the motivic fabric and tapering gently off, slightly modifies the cadence:

The same method of planting the recapitulation midcourse of the subsiding cadence appears at the corresponding juncture in the first movement of Brahms' Second Symphony. The piece starts with a motive in the bass (Ex. 329, bar 1),

which appears unchanged in the bass of the little **retransition** before the repeat sign (Ex. 330, bar 8) :

In the final retransition, however, at the **end of the** development (Ex. 331), this first bar seems to have been **lost:**

Yet, it is not. Utterly hidden in a seemingly **insignificant** middle voice, the first trombone (bars 5, 6, 7, 8), it is im- bedded, telescoped into the structure of the flowing cadential harmonies, suggesting by the extended time values of **its**

three notes the "written out ritardando".

What an enchanting, admirable subtlety!

Less concealed, yet equally delightful appears the same scheme in Ex. 330.

The end-and-beginning contraction of the joints appears sometimes reduced to the very instant of the contact. Ex. 332 shows a string of such "touch-and-go"s (market by $+$) and their constructive, impelling effect.

Brahms, Quartet Op. 51 No. 2

Examples 326 to 332 have in common the principle of advancing an approaching section (theme) to a point sooner than expected, thereby playing on the sensation of surprise. In examples 326 to 331 the entrance of the new section is wedged into the still progressing cadence, as diagrammed below (333a). In Ex. 332, the adjoining sections coincide tangentially (by way of deceptive cadences), as diagrammed in 333b.

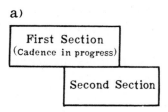

333.

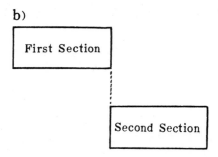

In the following we shall show methods of joining sections by a sort of *reversed* procedure. The psychological motive of surprise is now replaced by the one of preparedness. The oncoming section is properly invited, carefully announced, formally ushered in. The two sections are molded, almost welded together by the use of the second section's theme (or part of it) *before* its actual entrance, as a smooth and pleasant vehicle to lead into it.

Frequently, this is done by way of sequences, coming up from below, or down from above to the proper level of the so introduced theme.

334.

Mozart, Jupiter Symphony, Trio of the Menuetto

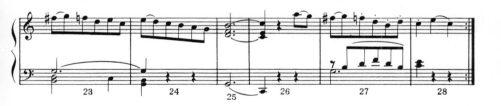

The above example (334) demonstrates this idea in the simplest form. Bars 17-22 consist of three sequences, each of them featuring one dominant-seventh chord and its natural

resolution. Measures 17-20 mediate between the preceding
and the following sections by retaining the rhythmical pulsation in an attenuated form, and dropping it altogether in
bar 21, thus disclosing the bare harmonies of the motif. Bars
21 and 22 act as the pivot between the abandonment of the
sequences and the entrance of the restatement.

In the following example, this pivot is represented by
bars 8 and 9 of the retransition. The passage, while showing
a highly artistic, contrapuntally rich tissue, is otherwise built
according to the same principle.

Brahms, Quartet Op. 51 No. 2

Even in fugal writing where unprepared entrances **of** the theme prevail because of their enhanced plasticity, the interludes sometimes usher in the theme by anticipatory sequences of its incipient motif (Ex. 336, 337, 338).

336.

Bach, Well-tempered Clav. I, Fugue 2
(Theme)

337.

(Theme)

338.

(Theme)

An intermediate mode between pure sequences and pure

cadences is used in transitions like Ex. 339 and 340b.

While part of the roundness and pleasantness here **rests**
in the fact that we are led smoothly *back* to a theme already
familiar from previous parts of the respective compositions
("restatement"), we can be just as pleasantly led *forward*
into a new theme, heard for the first time, a theme that

grows out of a motif pertaining to the transition itself. Thus for instance the "second theme" of a sonata may be foreshadowed:

Mozart, Symphony No. 38 (K. No. 504)

We do not know whether the composer preconceived his second theme (Ex. 341) and tried to introduce it by retrospective adaptation, or whether the little flourish, adorning

in threefold repetition the preceding cadential chords, actually inspired and prompted the theme. Nor is such speculation any of our business. In any case, there it is, alive and
delightful; and in any case we get the indubitable impression
that the lovely theme *did* spring forth from the tiny, unpre-
tentious arabesque.

In a similar way the second theme of Beethoven's first
Piano Sonata (Ex. 342, bar 13) resumes the thread of the
preceding "bridge passage".

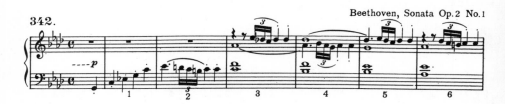

A closer examination of this bridge passage reveals that
it is organically linked to the contiguous sections *at both
ends*. For not only does it, at its own termination (bars 8-12),
foreshadow the new theme, but it evolves by spinning forth
the end of the preceding first theme (bar 2), using the little
motif in imitative style as a vehicle for the forthcoming
modulation (bars 3, 4, 5, 6).

Thus connecting links of any sort can originate by spinning forth the last musical idea, the last ramification of a terminating phrase.

It is natural that in such cases the beginning of the whole phrase (like bar 1 in Ex. 342) be dropped, and the molding be concentrated on the last motif (bars 3-6). Yet the same procedure of skipping the first motif and using only the second may also with advantage and added charm be applied to *introductory* links, like retransitions. Such a retransition, in contrast to examples 339-342, would not foreshadow the very beginning of the theme, but its immediate continuation, the second bar or so. We see this method applied to the retransition of the same Beethoven Sonata:

Here the motif is still more abridged than in the bridge passage of Ex. 342; in fact it is reduced almost to a grace-note figure. Skipping the first bar of the recapitulation (Ex. 343, bar 9), the little motif refers to the second bar (10). Note also how the pitch of the little figure in the theme itself (bar 10) is avoided before, so as to save its full effect for bar 10, while the upper line of the chain (bars 4, 6, 8) is gradually approaching this final pitch by stepwise descending sequences.

Similarly, in Ex. 344, it is the motive in the bass of the *second* bar of the theme (bar 6 of the example) that holds the lead among the motifs which, contrapuntally interwoven, make up the preceding retransition (bars 1, 2, 3, 4):

344.   Mozart, Symphony G minor (K 550) Andante

The following example presents an epitome of various ways of joining and molding together, as previously discussed.

345. Allegretto Grazioso

Brahms, Second Symphony

The movement starts with an eight bar phrase, ending on the dominant in the good old fashion. Even the suspension-resolution character of the two chords in bar 8 is familiar to us from innumerable encounters in classical music. Bar 9 repeats the formula, as if casually and haphazardly. Yet the idea of *spinning forth* the tiny motif of the upper voice gradually consolidates in bars 9-11, increasing each time the propelling power of the motif through changing harmonic interpretation. Now the vanishing spark of bar 8, gradually fanned through bars 9 and 10, flames up to new life. Bar 11 acts as the pivot between the old and the new. Bars 8-11 correspond to the bridge-passage of the Beethoven Sonata (Ex. 342, bar 1-12) in that here, too, the bridge is linked organically at both ends to the neighboring sections; except that here the integration is more concise and telling. The new theme thus introduced provides contrast by shifting tonality and emotional intensification up to bar 20. There the arch bends back again, using descending sequences (bars 21, 22) for a link to the restatement in bar 23. This bar is again the pivot on which two abutting sections hinge.

At another reprise, later in the piece, the telescoping device as shown in Ex. 326, 328, 330, 331, is used (Ex. 346).

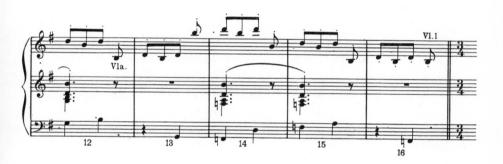

The process is still more telling here, in that the **broad** cadence, carrying the theme "pickaback" all the while, now almost fully coincides with the theme itself.

But the telescoping idea is much more firmly rooted here than by just the overlapping cadence as diagrammed in Ex. 333a. Harmony (the cadential progression) and melody (the dense motivic texture) combine to bind still closer the two adjacent sections.

The first section, approaching its end at this juncture, is marked by a motif in two-four time, appearing in the first ten bars of Ex. 346. The second section is marked by the main theme of the movement, starting in bar 17 at "Tempo primo". The intervening bars 11 through 16 represent the "joint".

The joint itself exhibits three layers. The uppermost, performed by violins and violas, continues the preceding section, bringing it to an end in bar 17. The middle layer, performed by woodwinds and horns, announces the on-coming main theme in a sparse and timid way, yet with sufficient distinctness. The motivic bridge is formed (1) by the sameness of the two upper pitches *b* and *d* of the wood-wind-chord; (2) by the sameness of instrumentation (the two oboes); (3) by shifting in bar 11 to a three-bar pattern which anticipates the triple meter of the ensuing theme; (4) by the *portamento* as indicated by the expression marks and the eighth rests at the end of bars 11, 12, 14, 15. All these means make the connection of this middle layer with the ensuing restatement (in which it becomes the upper layer) unmistakable. Just as unmistakable is, finally, the con-nection of the lowermost layer of the "joint"—the pizzicato figure in the cello—with the ensuing main part in which this instrumental group resumes its initial accompanying role in the smoothest and most natural manner, the changed notes now dictated by the harmonic requirements of the progressing cadence. If the highest note of this figure is omitted and replaced by a rest at the down-beats of bars 13 and 16, it is done so as to leave the register clear for the eighth-note motif in the strings (violas here) which at the same time link the two outermost layers in a fleeting contact.

Thus the smooth operation of the transition is three-foldly ensured. In the perfection of the *joint* we feel the skill of the *joiner,* tenoning and mortising, clinching and riveting the material of his creation. In *putting together* the proper parts in a proper way, he becomes the com - poser.

In the photoplay technique, adjoining scenes are connected either by "cuts" or by "dissolves". With a "cut" scenes follow each other sharply and without a transition. The "dissolve" uses an overlapping method, fading out one scene while the next simultaneously fades in, so that for a short while we see both pictures superimposed. Ex. 346 may be compared to such a dissolve. Bars 1 through 10 show the "picture" of the preceding section, approaching its end, but still "in the clear". In the clear, too, is the following section from bar 17 on, while bars 11 through 16 represent the "dissolve". In the same degree as the departing section (carried on by the upper layer of the violins and violas) fades out and loses significance, the arriving section of the lower layers fades in and gains significance. We notice that the composer indicated a *pp* for the upper string group, and at the same time a *p* for the part of the wind instruments (bar 11). The careful conductor will take this indication rather as a gradual *decrescendo* for the upper strings, to go along with a gradual, if light, *crescendo* for the wind group during the six bars of the dissolve (the latter followed by a *p dolce* again in bar 17).

Another surprising variant is provided in the next reprise (Ex. 347).

347.

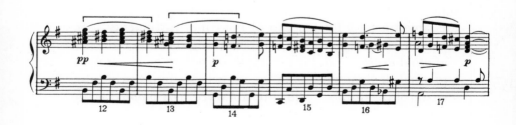

The theme enters here in the key of F♯ major, carried there by a preceding modulation. Bars 8, 9, 10, 11 of Ex. 347 obviously correspond to the same bars of Ex. 345. But while there the upper part is retained with changing harmonies, here the harmonization is retained, with changing upper part. The melody in bar 11 continues sequentially, with abridged and shifted rhythmical pattern (indicated by ⌐¬ ⌐¬), the sequence smoothly gliding *in the middle of its course* to the familiar key and theme (bar 14).

CHAPTER XII

THE FORMATIVE INFLUENCE OF MOVEMENT

The various methods of joining tend to polish and smooth the edges of adjoining sections. They tend to conceal the gaping seams that obtain in primitive adherence to conventional formulas of structure. But most of all they make for unbroken flow, for continuous *movement,* and prevent faltering and stagnation.

Stagnation is the worst enemy of form; and since form and inspiration are so intimately interrelated, we may well say that stagnation is the worst enemy of inspiration. If inspiration dies, form is doomed to die with it. What keeps them alive, is essentially *movement.* Movement is far more than just a sign of life; indeed, it is *"the very essence of life".*

It is a blessed wisdom of the English and French languages to call a complete division of a sonata or symphony a "movement". Thus in a terse way the product is identified with its most essential source. The Italian language also intimates the idea by calling such a section "Tempo".

But this continuous movement has little to do with inanely rolling sixteenths such as may be found in cheap "perpetuum mobile" compositions, full of empty sequences, or similar attempts at futile tone painting. Nor has the flow of a musical piece anything to do with speed. It applies to the slowest tempo as well as to the fastest.

As a model illustration of such unbroken flow I want to mention the Scherzo of Mendelssohn's "Midsummernights Dream" music—the most magnificent scherzo of our literature, not excepting Beethoven. So incessant is the torrent of this music that the composer just could not afford to interrupt it by inserting the obligatory "Trio". A composer knowing *the forms* would have added it. Its composer, knowing FORM, had to omit it.

Manifold are the means of keeping a composition in flow.

Take Prelude VI, in *d* minor, from the first volume of Bach's "Well-tempered Clavichord". The sweeping vitality of the piece, its unbroken flow, is brought about by the maintenance of a tiny triplet motif which pervades the entire piece, filling its arteries, as it were, with a homogeneous blood-substance.

Now take the first movement of Bach's "Italian Concerto". Here, too, there certainly is no danger of stagnation, as ever with Bach. But as to the propelling motor that keeps the movement moving, the piece appears somehow diametrically contrasting to the previously quoted *d* minor Prelude. For here, apart from the concluding section which rounds off the form, and apart from occasional motivic references, we see the thematic material constantly renewing itself in abounding richness, as if drawn from an inexhaustible cornucopia. Technical device is almost completely superseded by sheer inspiration — in truth, the best device of all!

The two pieces, reaching the common goal—unbroken flow—by opposite means, stand for innumerable other examples of their respective types. With regard to the maintenance of movement by motivic treatment, they represent the two extremes between which this kind of treatment varies —perpetuation of one motif, and accumulation of various motifs.

At any rate, the chief pervading principle is again: Avoid the worst enemy of form — stagnation!

Stagnation means the slackening or even breaking of the thread of musical narration.

If the concert-hall audience bursts into premature applause, taking a pronounced full cadence for the end of the piece, it is never their fault; rather is it wholly and solely the fault of the composer, and only he, not the audience, should feel embarrassed and punished. That will occasionally happen even with the greatest masters of the classical period, who sometimes were trapped in the routine of certain formal prototypes of which the average listener is innocent and ignorant. It will, however, not happen with Bach, who fortunately lived and created before formalism of stereotyped structure could congeal, and who therefore was able to follow his superior form-instinct, unhampered by the hazards of ingrained sonata-routine. Nor will it happen with Brahms, whose refined taste and subtlety, in revision of his predecessors' habits, rejected the conspicuously exposed seams of the conventional structure.

Another source of the stagnation danger lies in the opposite direction. It concerns the attenuation of the thread of narration by drawing it out excessively.

Conciseness makes for flow, protraction is apt to reduce flow to a trickle.

Mere cuts may help sometimes; but in other instances, especially with compositions of a finer and more intricate texture, mere cuts will not do, but must be supplemented by skilfully repairing the texture. (The effect of contraction on unbroken flow with respect to the *joints* was touched upon in Ex. 326-347).

The stagnating effect of protraction is often reducible to repetitiousness.

There is a peculiar thing about repetition in music. Music by and large is almost inconceivable without repetition. It is the rhythmical recurrence of a motivic pattern that provides the unifying undercurrent of sections, at least, if not of whole movements. Besides, we welcome the recurrence of themes as another means of unification and formal support to musical structure. And yet we are apt to take for mere repetition what the master, in pursuit of continuous flow, may present in constantly changing appearance, giving us just enough of the repetition to enjoy the acquaintance, and at the same time just enough of variation to enjoy subconsciously the constant renewal.

How many musicians or music lovers, who have heard, played or conducted Mozart's popular G Minor Symphony uncounted times and believe they know "every bar of it", would volunteer to reproduce extempore the second theme of its last movement?

There is nothing particularly tricky about this theme; on the contrary, we recollect it as a simple theme, built in regular period structure.

An eight bar phrase evidently recurs four times in the statement, and as many times, transposed into the original key of *g* minor, in the restatement.

Here are the eight "repetitions":

348 a)

Mozart, Symphony K. No. 550

Which is "the theme"? Each of the eight phrases could be it, and each a variant of each. Apparently alike for the listener, they are all different, considerably and delightfully different, even to the linking bars of the transitions. With such an unlimited supply of new ideas no stagnation can arise.

Motif and theme

If we compare bars 7 and 23 of Ex. 348b, we see that the bass of 23 slightly varies the bass of bar 7, in that it replaces the mere repetition of the d by alternating it with its neighbor tone, $c\sharp$. The same little bass figure appears also in the corresponding bar 23 of 348a; but while it has no further consequences there, here it is picked up and imitated in the following bars. Yet such imitations, commonplace in the province of counterpoint, become ever so much more than a contrapuntal sport in the domain of FORM. They keep movement rolling by the alternate emergence and submergence of the motif. The little motif of bar 23 (Ex. 348b), submerged here, emerges in bar 24, at the same time serving as an introduction to the theme. Submerging in bars 25 and 26, it emerges again in bars 27 and 28 as a new, varied continuation of the theme, during which, in turn, the beginning of the theme submerges into the tenor voice of bars 27 and 28. Thus counterpoint becomes *functional.* It assumes a real and quite essential formative function in that it exercises a *propelling force.*

No motif is too small, too insignificant, too negligible to promote, not only construction and movement, but inspiration itself, as is apparent in this last phrase. No motif is insignificant enough to be discarded for that reason.

Every combination of a few tones is apt to become a

motif and, as such, to pervade and feed the cellular tissue of a composition, emerging and submerging alternately, giving and receiving support and significance by turns. It revives and animates, and is revived and animated, in a continuous cycle of give and take. It lives on repetition and yet on constant metamorphosis; metamorphic, polymorphic, opalescent in itself, it takes on the hue, the flavor, the very mood of the environment in which it is imbedded. It smoothes and ruffles, it soothes and arouses; it bridges and reconciles, glues and splices, planes and levels, polishes and varnishes. But above all, it creates and feeds movement, movement, movement, *the very essence of life,* and fends off the arch-enemy, stagnation, the very essence of death.

It, the little motif, becomes the motive, the motive power, the MOTOR.

In Ex. 349 the theme starts with a weightless, introductory figure in the bass (bar 1). We have already dealt with this figure in another connection (Ex. 329-331). Now let us examine the first main section of this movement, including the first theme and transition passage, up to the second theme (Ex. 349).

349. Allegro ma non troppo   Brahms, Sec. Symphony Op.73, first mvt.

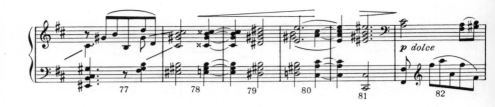

In listening to the beginning of this movement, our
main attention is taken up by the serene and noble lines in
horns and woodwinds (bars 2 to 20) which make the little
introductory motif of the string basses (bar 1) appear still
more insignificant. It gradually gains weight by repetition
(bars 5, 9, 13) until its functional part in the organism is
established, though the listener—absorbed by the events of
the upper voices, the real "theme"—is still hardly conscious
of its existence.

In bars 35 and 39 the motif emerges from its subdued
role, loftily exposed now to our attention; and it is now that
we consciously or half-consciously begin to link it with the
first bar of the piece, as its tender reverberation.

Its augmented appearance in bars 42 and 43 makes the
effect of a written out ritardando, thus announcing the advent of something new. This something new—the "transition
section"—indeed starts in bar 44.

But how? Again it is the same three tones of the motif
that connect the two sections. Yet, having been held back
by the augmented time-values, the motif (showing rhythmical elasticity as discussed on page 98ff) now releases a row
of quick, resilient tones which create a more lively and animated mood.

The motif has entered its first metamorphosis.

The animation is increased by a fourfold stretto, the

motif chasing itself through bars 52, 53, 54, 55. The momentum so gained leads to a temporary climax (59) in which the
motif, in lieu of the displaced theme, obtains complete, if
temporary, sovereignty. Appearing now in different registers
(59, 61, 63), it performs the modulation pertinent to the
transition section. Bars 64 and 65 reveal it splitting the bar
in two halves by its own reduction to half time. Here it
undergoes its second metamorphosis which is quickly to be
followed by another one in bar 66. Though the actual tones
of the upper voice in this bar (66) do not differ from the
two preceding bars, it is most of all the woodwind staccato,
as against the preceding string legato, that brings about a
complete change in mood. The motif has now taken on a
pronounced *scherzando* character. If compared with its first
occurrence in bar 1, it appears now almost unrecognizably
disguised.

At the same time, however, it is in a way more closely
connected with its original form than in the completely un-
disguised versions in bars 35, 39, 42-43. There it comprises
actually the three notes of the first bar. From bar 59 on, however, it also embraces the following bar, as expressed by the
leap of a fourth, up or down, according to the tonic-domi-
nant relation. Thus measures 59-60 correspond to 1-2, as do
61-62 and 63-64. From 66 on measures 9-10, or 13-14, serve
as a model. The added tone, the fourth tone of the figure,
becomes more and more essential in that it changes the silhouette of the motif. In bar 71 and thereafter, the outer
frame of this silhouette is all that is left of it. With these last
remnants it tapers off, completely fading out in bar 78.

So it is not the first theme, but the little introductory
motif that actually feeds the whole section from its rise in
the first bar to its expiration at the threshold of the second

theme.

Needless to say, its play is resumed and still more rami-
fied in the development section up to its submersion as
shown in Ex. 331, and again in the recapitulation and coda.
There it lingers, interwoven with other motifs, and finally
speaks the last word of the dying movement, as it spoke the
first, in the beginning (Ex. 350):

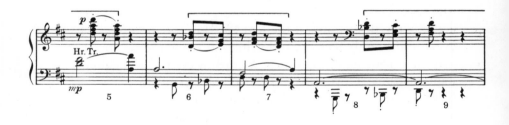

Again the motif appears in both the three-tone (bars 1-3) and the four-tone (6-10) form; besides, it appears in stretto (1-3), as introduced in the (here omitted) development section. In its longer form (6-10), its relation to the beats is shifted, providing another change which makes itself palpably felt and avoids mere repetition. In these bars (6-10) it circumplays the last echoing reminiscences of the main theme, which is also reduced here, like a dying spark, to the fragmentary size of a motif.

Still, we are much more conscious of the theme, in spite of its fragmentary size, than of the circumplaying motif. And we are more conscious of the theme in spite of its scattered and intermittent presences than we are of the omnipresent, flowing, rolling motif.

For the theme announces and asserts its presence (compare the entrance of the second theme in bar 82, Ex. 349); the motif sneaks in and sneaks out, and meanwhile travels and meanders, unobtrusively and under the surface, as it were.

The theme is sizable, clearly shaped and clean cut; it has its countenance, its character, its mood. The motif is loose jointed, limber, flexible and versatile; it plays in a thousand colors and assimilates a thousand moods.

The theme strides and poses, stamping its seal on our mind, while underneath the nimble motif glides and flits and all but escapes our attention.

The theme cannot force its weight through the delicate veins and ramifications of the cellular texture, which the swift and fluid motif easily penetrates.

Look at a building. You cannot overlook the doors, windows and balconies, all in proper place and position.

But of little avail would be their proper place and position, were it not for the *building material*—the handy, adaptable bricks that fill the space between them, surrounding, supporting, cementing them, keeping them properly together and properly apart.

In Ex. 349 we viewed a section of such a façade, made up mostly of the building material between the first theme and the second, of which we indicated only the first bar (82). We pursued the motif through its various metamorphoses from its origin to its expiration. Could we have missed anything? Let us see.

When the motif is brought to full focus in bar 59, we see it accompanied by what appears to be a broken harmony in a lower voice. Nothing in particular seems to distinguish this harmonic support of the motif, except that the breaking of the chord reveals a certain pattern. This pattern repeats in bar 61, with the registers of the voices interchanged, and again in bar 63 with registers restored. By now we feel that the pattern of the broken harmony, meant to be an accompaniment at first, is on the way to establishing itself motivically. This feeling grows with bars 66-67 when the two motifs, bound together at first, begin to separate from one another. This separation asserts itself in the two following sequences (bars 68-71), at the same time emphasizing the independence of the two motifs. With bar 71, the first motif is reduced to the extremes of its silhouette, leaving the field —and the task of propulsion— to the second motif. The few remaining bars (up to 78) show the first motif submerging in the same degree as the second motif simultaneously emerges, approaching again the "dissolve" technique of Ex. 346. When the second theme, after a few bars of transition,

starts (82), the first motif is definitely dropped and replaced by the second motif, which accompanies the second
theme for a while and, later on, gets lost in the course of the
following events.

Epitomizing this brief analysis: The pillars of this section as viewed so far are the two themes. The space between
them is occupied by building material. This building material is not sawdust and stuffing, but *live, organic fibre*. It is
made up of two motifs, independent of one another and of
the two themes, though the first motif is closely attached to
the first theme and the second motif is loosely attached to
the second theme. These two motifs relieve each other in
the course of the building process. However, this relief is
brought about not by juxtaposition but by overlapping and
gradual dissolve.

We are fully conscious of the themes whose distinguish-
ing mark is prominence and impressiveness, and whose function, architecturally and psychologically, is to act as the
salient landmarks of the composition.

We are only partly conscious of the motifs, whose mark
is *un*prominence and restraint, and whose invaluable function is to build, to cement, to keep life alive, to continue, to
promote and propel — all this in the service of that supreme
artistic demand, which is at the same time supreme artistic
benefactor: F O R M .

The thematic motif

As an aerolite may break from a heavenly body and
continue gyrating for a while by its own power, so may a
particle of the solid theme break away and, in motif manner,
circle around its generator (Ex. 351).

Mozart, String Quartet K. No. 465

It is not the contrapuntal device that constitutes the virtue of the "imitation" in bar 2 and later in bar 4 but its formative function, easily to be seen in the ensuing bars.

Activated by the last offshoot of the phrase, the figure, now a motif in itself, reactivates its source (bar 5, 1st vl.,) and persists in the cello, while the leading voice sings out its lyrical sequel. Splitting in half now, aerolite fashion again, the motif appears to taper off (10) ; yet, the split fragment rekindles the other voices (12) and they reflect the fragment, its tonal pattern imperceptibly changed now, in playful imitations. Again it flares up and in a last rise brings the passage to an end.

Again, the motif is as small and insignificant as can be. That is why it hardly enters our consciousness; yet, when listening to the melody of the leading voice in bars 6-11, we pleasantly, if unconsciously, feel its simultaneous generating function. This function is enhanced by the polyphonic, or semi-polyphonic setting.

Beethoven was not particularly polyphony-minded. His mind worked in other directions. Yet he, too, knew, or knew without knowing that he knew, the constructive value of the smallest, the most insignificant particle of a theme.

For that matter, what else should such a particle be but insignificant? Suppose you are admiring the exquisitely curved lines of a drawing. If you divide such a line into tiny particles, will not these fragments necessarily lose their prominence and grandeur? By the same token the most wonderful poem is composed of words which, individually, show no trace of uniqueness, but are bound to be used over and over again by the most prosaic mind in the most prosaic connection.

The first theme of Beethoven's Pastoral Symphony consists of four two-four bars (Ex. 352).

Short as this theme is, it contains enough material to feed no less than two thirds (to be exact, 337 out of 512 bars) of the movement. This material consists of a number of motifs, each equivalent to a bar, or even a half bar, of the theme. In contrast to Ex. 349, the diversities of the motifs here are not of rhythmical but of tonal nature, while the rhythm, the more essential motivic element, is retained. The composition shows that *nothing is wasted;* that nothing is too small to form a cell of the structure and to maintain the smooth, undulating flow.

Due to the almost completely homophonic style of the composition, the motifs do not form an undercurrent here, but always constitute the leading voice, though sometimes in lower registers. Thus they can easily be exhibited detached, in one voice (Ex. 353-367).

352.   (theme)

353.  (motif: bar 2)

354. (3)

355. (3)

356. (1)
(transition)

357. (2 or 3)
(part of second theme)

358.

(closing group)   (same)

359.

(codetta)   (same)

360.

(retransition)   (1)

361.

(development)   (2

362.

                                                     (2, whole and half)

*(development continues the same way in the keys of G and E for another
40 measures.)*

363. (2)

364. (2)

(Still development.) Follows recapitulation unfolding all the material again.

365. (half of 2 or 3)

Only in two places, the motifs show a rhythmical variation to triplets: (Ex. 366, 367)

366.

(variant of Ex. 358)

367.

(variant of Ex. 365)

The confinement of the motif material to the leading voice, and the resulting absence of a fine-spun, motivically interwoven texture, make this kind of composition appear simple almost to the point of primitivity, if contrasted to the subtle artistry of Mozart or Brahms.

Does that mean fault or virtue? It certainly means both. One thing, however, is certain: If you want to study the *craft,* you had better enroll with Mozart.

CHAPTER XIII

BEGINNING AND ENDING

Having dealt so far mainly with the items conducive to
the structure and fluency of music *in progress,* let us now
look into the beginning and ending of a composition.

As a narrative may start either by plunging *medias in
res,* or by first creating an introductory general atmosphere
of location, time, situation, etc., or by a completely detached
introduction, prologue or preface; so may a musical narrative show different types of beginnings, roughly corresponding to those mentioned above.

Ex. 368-72 illustrate the "plunging *medias in res*" type.

R. Strauss, "Don Juan"

369.

R. Strauss, "Rosenkavalier"

370.

R. Strauss, "Salome"

371.

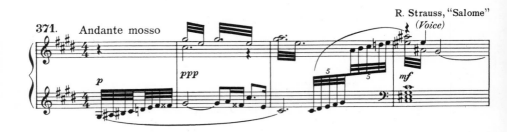

372.

In the prime of our classical music, composers liked to start a larger, especially a symphonic, piece with an introduction in slow tempo. This introduction usually was a completely detached statement, grave and austere in mood, sometimes also leading into the main part by direct motivic preparation (Ex. 373).

Sometimes it would assume the character of a vague improvisation, starting from afar (Ex. 374), or would start like a brewing mist, gradually dissipating and giving way to the bright light, as in Mozart's famous "Dissonant" Quartet (Ex. 375).

373.

374. Adagio

Beethoven, Overture No. 3, Leonore

375.

Mozart, Quartet K. No. 465

Adagio

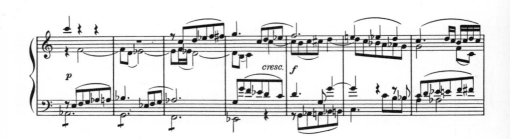

Beethoven started his first two symphonies with slow introductions, pretty much in the traditional style. To the revolutionary spirit and attitude of the third symphony, however, such an introduction would not fit. It would perhaps minimize this spirit rather than promote it. On the other hand, to put the first theme bluntly and nakedly at the beginning, would be equally unsatisfactory; for the theme, with all its greatness, lacks the dramatic bite of the *medias in res* type. Again Beethoven cut the Gordian knot by resorting to utter primitivity, and again this primitivity proved a blessed inspiration. The traditional "introduction" is reduced to two mere flashes of the tonic triad which open the wild chase of the movement (Ex. 376).

Beethoven, Third Symphony

The starting "from afar", as shown in Ex. 374, is not limited to the improvisational, detached introduction of a piece, but may just as well open the main theme itself (Ex. 377).

377.

This way of beginning creates a certain suspense and gives the opening, as it were, an obliquity which has to be straightened. The straightening is achieved when the tonic harmony is reached (Ex. 377, bar 6 and still more bar 8). In this moment, the suspense ceases and gives way to the feeling of assertion.

This type of opening has a particularly romantic character. No piece of Bach, or of his epoch, is known to me that would start otherwise than with the tonic triad, or, if in a single voice, with the tonic harmony suggested.

The suspense of the harmonic obliquity can be protracted considerably.

In Schumann's song "Mondnacht" (Ex. 378) the tonic triad, to be sure, occurs in bar 10; yet, accentless and subdued to the role of ushering in the powerful dominant half cadence (bar 13), it has no weight, no import of its own. It is not before bar 59 that the singing voice, at least, reaches its "home" (text: "als flöge sie *nach Haus*"—"as though it would fly *home*"). The full tonic effect, however, is still evaded by the deflection of the bass and the deceptive har-

monization of the accompaniment. Only two bars later, at
the downbeat of bar 61, the long yearned for assertion and
repose comes to pass, in the nick of time, when the whole
song is practically over.

It must be hoped that the reader feels the tremendous influence of this manner of expression on the FORM of the composition, the manner of expression being the distant beginning and long delayed arrival, and FORM the material realization of the spiritual image — another definition of FORM, if you like.

The most amazing example of this type presents itself in Schumann's "Fantasy", op. 17, first movement. The tripartite piece starts with oblique harmony and reaches the end of its first section (bar 128) without ever arriving at the tonic triad. It continues its restless travels through constantly changing keys, moods, material, with no reference anywhere to the main key. No sooner than in bar 308—13 bars before the end of the piece—the "arrival" announces itself, spreading throughout these last 13 bars, the final repose still delayed by ever so pungent retardations up to the very end. The wide-stretched arch of the piece may be likened to Lindbergh's nonstop flight from New York to Paris in 1927, or to the high-arched curve of a star shooting through the whole celestial vault.

The ending of a musical piece, too, may show traits similar to those just discussed for the beginning.

If we spoke of a *medias in res* type, as shown in Ex. 368-372, we understood by that a beginning that would plunge into the narration point blank, without any ado. To this kind of a beginning would correspond a kind of ending also point blank, without any ado, the narration carried up to the last word, or bar, or sound; and after that no word wasted. If there were such a term as "mediis ex rebus", it would be the corresponding term.

Here are a few examples of this type (379-385):

379. Mozart, Symphony K.N. 543 *(Finale)*

(Theme)

380.  Mozart, Quartet K.N. 464 *(Finale)*

 *(Theme)*

(appearing here in 2nd violin)

381.  Mozart, Quartet K.N. 465 *(Finale)*

382.  Brahms, Piano-Quintet Op. 34 *(Finale)*

In most instances (Ex. 379, 380, 383-385) the thematic material is used up to the last bar or sound. In some instances, the theme is just in time to catch up with the last chord (Ex. 379, 380, 384, 385). In other instances, the theme, or motif, is even late, and its extreme tip still protrudes beyond the concluding chord (Ex. 381, 382). With these endings, a composition brims over with real substance; so much so that out of the very closing phrase its subject, or theme, could be reconstructed.

It would certainly be difficult to reconstruct any thematic substance out of a "closing phrase" like the following, which may illustrate the preceding idea by contrast (Ex. 386):

The reader may object: Though certainly a contrast, why must it be laid on so thick, artificially and superfluously?

With grief it must be stated that this example is not made up fictitiously. It is a literal quotation, a quotation, in fact, from the most popular of the classical symphonies. Here primitivity, a blessing in so many other instances, turns into a perfect nightmare. To be sure, these 41 last bars of Beethoven's Fifth Symphony are lead up to by other preceding bars. Yet no other brain would have contrived this peculiar chariot to carry a conductor (any conductor) to the triumph of a glory-bedecked hero. It leads one to believe the current story of one such conductor who, jerked around prematurely by the frenzied cheers of a hypnotized audience that just could not restrain its ecstasy any longer, quickly bowed to the raging masses and, wheeling back again was just in time to deal, a victorious gladiator, the deadly finishing stroke.

If Ex. 379-382 represent an accelerating type of conclusion, Ex. 386 shows the antipode of this type, namely the retarding, broadening type of conclusion, in its most primitive form, brought about by the hypnotic effect of excessive repetition. Other and nobler illustrations of the retarding conclusion are shown in Ex. 387-390.

387. Adagissimo   Bach, Organ-Toccata D minor

388. Adagio Bach, W. Cl. I, Prelude 2

Allegro

389.

Bach, W. Cl. I, Fugue 1

390.

Bach, W. Cl. I, Prelude 8

The endings in these examples, as compared with Ex. 379-382, are no longer precipitous. They do not assert themselves by pounding the tonic profusely; on the contrary, the relieving final harmony of the tonic appears now reserved for the very last sound. Before that, the harmonies grope their way in spreading ramifications like those of a huge river delta. As the waters of the delta, struggling along in the last phase of their journey, follow the irresistible call of Mother Ocean, so these harmonies, straying in desperate agony of search, call for acceptance and are called into acceptance by Mother Tonic.

This effect is particularly stressed if the tonic is planted in the bass long before the close and is sustained there up to the end as a "pedal point". It attracts the other voices like a magnet until it embraces and absorbs them in the tonic triad. (Ex. 388-390). This final triad makes the effect of inexorable consummation of Destiny, and at the same time of the longed for peace and consolation.

The following poem by Goethe may perhaps serve as a linguistic analogy.

Wanderers Nachtlied

Der du von dem Himmel bist,
Alles Leid und Schmerzen stillest,
Den, der doppelt elend ist,
Doppelt mit Erquickung füllest,
Ach, ich bin des Treibens müde!
Was soll all der Schmerz und Lust?
Süsser Friede,
Komm, ach komm in meine Brust!

The Wanderer's Night Song

Thou who comest from on high,
Who all woes and sorrows stillest,
Who, for twofold misery,
Hearts with twofold balsam fillest,
Would this constant strife would cease!
What are pain and rapture now?
Blissful peace,
To my bosom hasten thou!

(*English version by E. A. Bowring*)

Does not the "Thou" of the first line which sustains the "keynote" up to the last line, resemble the pedal point of the tonic? Does not the parenthesis of lines 5 and 6 in its complete detachment correspond to the harmonically detached "straying" voices over the pedal point? And the last two lines, consummating the invocation of the preposed "Thou", to the final triad which also consummates the call of the preposed keynote? And even spiritually, does not the final triad (especially in Ex. 390) likewise suggest the appeal to the great Comforter, Peace?

What has been said and shown here on the subject of form, is by no means meant to be a comprehensive theory. In fact it is a tiny, perhaps an infinitesimal part of it.

Though the examples for demonstration have been chiefly chosen from the classical literature, as part of the general musical consciousness, more accessible and traceable for that reason, the *formative principles* shown at work are not bound to any particular style or epoch or idiom. Even where tonality and key have a bearing, for instance in the relation of tension and attraction between secondary steps and tonic, it is the unchangeable *effect* which is aimed at, not the changeable and constantly changing *means*.

Sometimes we may have made a statement the opposite of which may be equally true. This fact does not render the knowledge and application of *either one* less useful and desirable. If all paths lead to Rome, it is still good to know them all and remain the master of one's own choice. If the proverb is taken literally, the consideration of all circumstances involved may lead to an "opposite" choice, or anyone in between. The same holds good if the proverb is taken figuratively. One should know the ways in order to be able to try them out and arrive at an ultimate choice. It remains largely unknown how many sketches the master may have rejected before arriving at the expression that seems so natural and unquestionable to the naive listener.

In any narrative—epic, dramatic or musical—every word or tone should be like a soldier marching towards the one, common, final goal: *conquest of the material.* The way the artist makes every phrase of his story such a soldier, serving to unfold it, to support its structure and development, to build plot and counterplot, to distribute light and shade, to point incessantly and lead up gradually to the climax, in short the way every fragment is impregnated with its mission towards the whole, makes up this delicate and so essential objective which we call F O R M.

ABOUT THE AUTHOR

Ernst Toch was born December 7, 1887 in Vienna. Growing up in a family puzzled by his musical proclivities and unfavorable to his obsession with composing he was left entirely to himself. In his early teens he copied Mozart's ten famous String Quartets and Bach's "Welltempered Clavichord". It taught him what, in his own words, no living teacher ever could have taught him. While he was still in High School, his "A Minor Quartet" was performed by the Rosé Quartet of Vienna (1905). Other quartets followed in quick succession and were performed by the leading European groups. His musicianship as yet unacknowledged by his family, Toch studied medicine for two years at the University of Vienna. In 1909, after being awarded one of the most substantial scholarships for composition (Mozart Prize, Frankfurt am Main) he could reorient his life and work towards music exclusively. In 1913 he was called to teach composition at the Hochschule für Musik in Mannheim, Germany. From 1915 to 1918 he served in the Austrian army, at both the Russian and Italian fronts. After the war, he returned to Mannheim, resuming composing and teaching. In 1929 he moved to Berlin, having now become one of the leading figures in contemporary music, whose works had brought him international recognition. He first came to the United States in 1932 when he toured the country under the auspices of Pro Musica Society. In 1934 he was invited to teach at the New School for Social Research in New York, where he remained until 1936. From 1940 on, he taught at the University of Southern California at Los Angeles. In 1940 he became a citizen of the United States.

A reference list of his principle works follows:

ORCHESTRA: Phantastische Nachtmusik op. 27 (*Tischer & Jagenberg, Cologne*), Concerto for Piano and Orchestra op. 38 (*Schott, Mainz*), Divertimento for Wind Instruments op. 39 (*Schott*), Comedy for Orchestra op. 42 (*Schott*), Fanal for Orchestra and Organ op. 45 (*Schott*), Motley Suite op. 48 (*Schott*), Little Theater Suite op. 54 (*Schott*), Music for Orchestra and Baritone op. 60 (*Schott*), Symphony for Piano and Orchestra op. 61 (*Schott*), "Big Ben", a Variation Phantasy on the Westminster Chimes, op. 62 (*Associated Music Publishers, New York*), "Pinocchio", a Merry Overture (*Assoc. Mus. Publ.*), Prelude to a Fairy Tale (*Schott*), Overture "The Fan" (*Schott*), Paraphrase on Mozart's Variations "Unser dummer Pöbel meint" for Orchestra and Piano concertante (*Delkas, Los Angeles*), "Hyperion", a Dramatic Prelude op. 71 (*Delkas*)

CHAMBER ORCHESTRA: "The Chinese Flute", a Chamber Symphony with Soprano Solo op. 29 (*Schott*), Dance Suite op. 30 (*Schott*), Five Pieces op. 33 (*Schott*), Concerto for Cello and Chamber Orchestra op. 35 (*Schott*)

CHAMBER MUSIC: Stringquartet a minor op. 12, Stringquartet g major op. 15, Stringquartet d flat major op. 18 (*J. Weinberger, Leipzig*), Serenade for three Violins op. 20 (*Weinberger*), Serenade for two Violins and Viola op. 25 (*Tischer & Jagenberg, Delkas*), Stringquartet c major op. 26 (*Tischer & Jagenberg*), Stringquartet on the name "Bass", op. 28 (*Tischer & Jagenberg*), Stringquartet op. 34 (*Schott*), Divertimento for Violin and 'Cello, op. 37a (*Schott*), Divertimento for Violin and Viola op. 37b (*Schott*), Sonata for Violin and Piano op. 44 (*Schott*), Sonata for 'Cello and Piano op. 50 (*Schott*), Quintet for Piano and Strings op. 64 (*Delkas*), "Poems to Martha", Quintet for Strings and Baritone op. 66 (*Delkas*), Stringquartet op. 70 (*Delkas*) .

PIANO: Burlesken op. 31 (*Schott*), Three Piano Pieces op. 32 (*Schott*), Capriccetti op. 36 (*Schott*), Dance and Play Pieces op. 40 (*Schott*), Sonata op. 47 (*Schott*), Echoes from a Small Town op. 49 (*Schott*), Ten Concert Etudes op. 55 (*Schott*), Ten Recital Etudes op. 56 (*Schott*), Ten moderately difficult Etudes op. 57 (*Schott*), Ten Simple Etudes op. 58 (*Schott*), Ten Beginners' Etudes op. 59 (*Schott*), "Profiles" op. 68 (*Assoc. Mus. Publ.*), "Ideas" op. 69 (*Delkas*)

SONGS: Nine Songs for Soprano and Piano op. 41 (*Schott*)

CANTATAS: "Das Wasser", Cantata for Tenor, Baritone, Chorus, small Orchestra and Narrator op. 53 (*Schott*), "Cantata of the Bitter Herbs", for Choir, Soli, Orchestra and Narrator, op. 65

STAGE WORKS: "The Princess on the Pea", a Musical Fairy Tale in one act, op. 43 (*Schott*), "The Fan", Opera Capriccio in three acts op. 51 (*Schott*), "Egon and Emilie", Music Sketch op. 46 (*Schott*)

RECORDINGS: "Pinocchio", a Merry Overture (Fr. Stock with Chicago Symphony Orchestra; *Columbia*), Piano Quintet op. 64 (Kaufman Quartet and Composer; *Columbia*), "The Chinese Flute" op. 29 (Pacific Symphonietta, Man. Compinsky cond.; *Alco, Los Angeles*) "The Covenant" (part of "Genesis", Werner Janssen cond.; *Artist Records*), Piano Quintet op. 64 (American Art Quartet and Composer; *Alco*), Serenade for two Violins and Viola op. 25 (Kaufman Trio; *Vox*), Poems to Martha op. 66 (Compinsky group; *Alco*), Piano Sonata op. 47 (composer; *Alco*), Stringquartet op. 70 (London Stringquartet; *Alco*) Album of Piano Pieces (composer; *Alco*).

INDEX OF NAMES PAGE

DATE DUE